KV-512-421

CONTENTS

MARK GET

TO

THEIR
FINEST HOUR

THEIR FINEST HOUR

**An Evocative Memoir of the
British People in Wartime 1939-1945**

ALAN KENDALL

WAYLAND (PUBLISHERS) LONDON

Text copyright © 1972 by Alan Kendall
First published in 1972 by
Wayland (Publishers) Limited
101 Grays Inn Road, London WC1
Printed in Great Britain by
C. Tinling & Co. Ltd, London and Prescot
SBN 85340 158 6

LIST OF ILLUSTRATIONS

(*Between pp.* 98 *and* 187)

5. "Let us go forward together" – poster showing Churchill.
6. "Back them up" – poster urging support for anti-aircraft forces.
7. Guinness advertisement.
8. A wartime newspaper seller.
9. Speaker at Hyde Park Corner, London.
10. Trial of conscientious objectors.
11. Anti-war poster.
12. Posters urging support for the Red Army.
13. "Lord Haw Haw", alias William Joyce.
14. B.B.C. newsreader.
15. Children dressed in uniform.

5. Feeding the Fighting Nation
1, 2, "Grow your own food" posters.
3. "Dig for Victory" poster.
4, 5. Ministry of Food recommended wartime diets.
6. Poster stressing virtues of vegetables.
7. Poster urging people to eat rabbits.
8. Officially approved ration packages.
9. Fruit seller amidst rubble of bomb-damaged London.
10. Three families solve the food problem by sharing their meal.
11. Sharing a "cuppa".
12. Sand-bagged restaurant – "Business as usual".
13. Advertisement for Bulmer's Cider.
14. Soldiers in canteen.
15. Shop selling prisoner-of-war parcels.
16. Unloading American eggs.

6. Women at War
1. The life of an airman's wife.
2. Women shopping.
3. Women emerge from public air-raid shelter.
4, 5. Female workers in factory.
6, 7. Women repairing tanks.
8. Women working the land.
9. Recruiting poster for Women's Land Army.
10. Women of the Womens' Auxiliary Air Force awarded for bravery.
11. Policewoman walking in the Strand, London.
12. Volunteer waitress takes soldiers' orders for lunch.
13. Members of the Womens' Voluntary Service look after evacuees.
14. Poster warning against VD.

7. Entertainment in Wartime
1. Queue outside a cinema.
2. Mae West, film star.
3. Leslie Howard, film star.
4. Producer Alec Clunes coaches cast for West End Play.
5. The impresario C. B. Cochrane's "Young Ladies" on stage.
6. Actor Leslie Henson.
7. Factory workers relax to chamber music.
8. Val Guilgud directs a B.B.C. play.
9. Comedian Tommy Handley next to a waxwork bust of him.
10. Vera Lynn, the forces' sweetheart.
11. A wartime night-club scene.

Introduction

In December, 1970, almost the whole of Britain experienced electricity cuts. As the nation lunched by candlelight one dark afternoon and listened to the one o'clock news, the broadcast finished with the words, "So it's back to the wartime slogan, 'Watch that light!'"

Several things sprang to mind at that moment. Odd, that more than twenty-five years after World War Two, a national power crisis should so evoke memories of that war. How sharply those who knew and survived that terrible war must be divided from those to whom it means nothing! Young people are often bored to death with their elders' tales of the war. But for older people, the emotional impact lingers on and even today has amazing vitality. For example Harold Wilson – as prime minister – tried to sell devaluation to the British people with a cheap reference on television to the "spirit of Dunkirk".

It seems a propitious moment, therefore, some twenty-five years after the close of World War Two, to take a longer look at what Winston Churchill described – and many have come to regard – as "their finest hour". Was it really a period of national heroism on an unprecedented scale? Does history bear this out? Can the British, normally a modest, even self-deprecating, people have for once had a moment of truth about themselves? Not all the episodes were glorious, as subsequent pages will reveal. Had Germany not postponed her invasion of Britain when she did, the story might have ended differently.

We will look primarily at the hectic twelve months from the German invasion of Western Europe in May, 1940, and the Battle of Britain, to the bombing of London – fiercest in September and October, and prolonged into May, 1941. The Battle of Britain and the Blitz represented a valiant victory, not only for a few brave fighter pilots, but for the people of London and of provincial areas which suffered a similar fate. An honourable victory was won, too, in the long and often desperate period of austerity ahead, in the years before peace finally came. Even now, not all the facts are known, although more become available each year with the release of official documents. Some can never be known, however. What follows is an attempt to put into perspective the events of that year by examining the fabric and texture of daily life as people waited for, and finally faced, the German attack.

About four weeks before the first heavy air attack abated, Winston Churchill said: "I see the damage done by the enemy attacks; but I also see, side by side with the devastation and amid the ruins, quiet, confident, bright and smiling eyes . . ." This was certainly true. What is doubtful is the conclusion he drew: ". . . beaming with a consciousness of being associated with a cause far higher and wider than any human or personal issue. I see the spirit of an unconquerable people." This was the rhetoric of war; it seems now that, far from espousing "high and wide causes" – particularly during the Blitz – people struggled simply to survive, to carry on, to keep going. After the long uncertain months of the "phoney war", the Blitz was a welcome relief to many, despite the death and destruction it entailed.

Remarkably little neurosis or mental disorder occurred during the Blitz. In the short term the Blitz might even have improved mental health. It completely discredited those experts who had predicted mass hysteria. On the contrary, there emerged a legendary spirit of solidarity – the sort of solidarity which made commuting stockbrokers throw off their jackets and help unload supplies for the injured and the homeless.

Winston Churchill chose to describe this as the spirit of an unconquerable people; in reality Britain's fate would rest on matters largely outside ordinary people's control. What Churchill saw at work was the spirit of people – pure and simple – liberated under crisis. True to human nature, that spirit died all too soon, once the crisis had been overcome. This is not to belittle it, for it was all the more remarkable in view of official failure to provide adequately for the people's welfare. From this point of view it certainly was "their finest hour".

The Historical Perspective

At 11.15 a.m. on Sunday, 3rd September, 1939, Prime Minister Neville Chamberlain broadcast to the British people and announced that the country was at war. The news hardly surprised anyone: indeed to many it was a relief. Mass Observation interviewers collected people's reactions to the news that morning, and the words "relief", "lifting of tension", "glad", and "thankful" were on everyone's lips. Almost at once the warning wail of a siren sounded. At first people thought that it was just an air raid rehearsal – ill timed, certainly, coming so soon after

Chamberlain's announcement. In fact it was a false alarm. A solitary aircraft straying from Le Touquet in France had been enough to alert the expectant defence system.

Since World War One the development of aircraft implied great dangers in any future war. As early as 1921 the Italian General Giulio Douhet had published a book entitled *The Command of the Air*, and although air raids had taken place in the 1914–18 war, relatively few civilians had actually experienced them. There was no national experience of air attack on which to draw for the future. But those with some knowledge of them never doubted that in the next war disaster would strike from the air far more terribly than it had ever done before.

In the event, the experts were expecting much worse than actually happened, by basing their calculations on what had occurred in the last war. Politicians too had been proclaiming doom and disaster. Clement Attlee said in October, 1935: "We believe that another world war will mean the end of civilization. Modern weapons are so dangerous that they cannot be left in the hands of national governments ...". And Stanley Baldwin, Churchill, Simon and Chamberlain all expressed similar fears in the years leading up to 1939. H. G. Wells' book *The Shape of Things to Come*, made into a film, proved to be a reasonably accurate forecast of the course of the war. If the government was really so pessimistic, then why was the country so badly equipped to face the air raids when they actually came?

However, twelve months were to pass from Britain's declaration of war on Germany to the unleashing of the full fury of the German air offensive on London. Looking back, one could see that events were building up to a climax. But those who lived through it may be forgiven if the first few months of the phoney – or "bore" – war lulled them into a false sense of security, or if they grew disenchanted. Of course many people had no illusions as to what the eventual outcome must be. When the German attack turned on the West in April and May of 1940, their fears were confirmed.

As early as 10th May large-scale German parachute landings were expected over London; security precautions, hitherto lax, were tightened. The German army reached the Channel coast of Europe on 20th May; the Belgian army capitulated. On 27th May the British Expeditionary Force began its evacuation from Dunkirk, to be completed on 3rd June.

A German invasion of England now seemed certain. *The Daily Mirror* called for a British attack, without really suggesting the means. Hitler seemed to think that if only he waited, Britain would beg for peace. But Britain underwent a change of Prime Minister – and a change of heart. Neville Chamberlain plainly no longer commanded confidence or respect, and King George VI had asked Winston Churchill to form a new government on 10th May. At the time of Dunkirk, the new Prime Minister, grimly declared: "We shall not flag or fail. We shall fight in France, we shall fight on the seas and oceans, we shall fight with growing confidence and growing strength in the air, we shall defend our island, whatever the cost may be, we shall fight on the beaches, we shall fight on the landing grounds, we shall fight in the fields and in the streets, we shall fight in the hills; we shall never surrender."

Events in Europe brought home Churchill's words. On 17th June Marshal Pétain told the French people, "*Il faut cesser la lutte*" – "We must give up the fight." Official French opposition to Germany was over. The army was to lay down its arms and the country was divided into an occupied zone and an unoccupied zone with its centre at Vichy. Next day Winston Churchill was again moved to oratory in the House of Commons: "Let us therefore brace ourselves to our duty and so bear ourselves that if the British Commonwealth and Empire lasts for a thousand years men will still say, 'This was their finest hour.'"

These were ringing words to stir the masses in such a dark moment. But as the diarist Harold Nicolson noted, in any other situation this kind of speech tended to sound false: "We listen to Winston Churchill on the wireless after dinner. He is a little too rhetorical, and I do not think that his speech will really have gone down with the masses. He is too belligerent for this pacifist age, and although once anger comes to steel our sloppiness, his voice will be welcome to them, at the moment it reminds them of heroism which they do not really feel." In January, 1940, few felt the need for heroism. In June they would have more reason. Reading Churchill's speeches, or listening to recordings of them now, one finds them extremely moving, even if their sentiments and expression are unfashionable. Although they were originally only delivered to a very select audience in the House of Commons – certainly the two speeches quoted here – they made an amazing national impact. After the 4th June speech Harold Nicolson was moved to call it "the finest speech that I have ever heard," and the "finest hour" speech of 18th June "magnificent".

When broadcast over the air, however, Nicolson thought the effect was very different: "How I wish Winston would not talk on the wireless unless he is feeling in good form. He hates the microphone, and when we bullied him into speaking last night, he just sulked and read his House of Commons speech over again. Now, as delivered in the House of Commons, that speech was magnificent, especially the concluding sentences. But it sounded ghastly on the wireless. All the great vigour he put into it seemed to evaporate." Cecil King, of *The Daily Mirror*, felt rather the same way: " ... a few stumbling sentences to the effect that the situation was disastrous but all right. Whether he was drunk or all-in from sheer fatigue, I don't know, but it was the poorest possible effort on an occasion when he should have produced the finest speech of his life." Was it not, then, the finest speech of his life? Sir Henry "Chips" Channon, who held Chamberlain in high regard almost to the point of infatuation, gives a terse, wry assessment of the speech: "I wasn't very impressed, but I suppose that the nation will be."

The nation was impressed and steeled itself to face its finest hour, but the critical moment still had not come. Days lengthened into weeks. British ports were bombed. June gave way to July, and still the expected invasion did not come. All through July and into early August the German Luftwaffe continued to bomb British shipping and ports, but not until 13th August did Hermann Goering order the air attack on Britain to begin. He had first to destroy R.A.F. Fighter Command, so as to clear the way for invasion or "Operation Sea Lion" as it was known to the Germans.

The facts about the Battle of Britain, as the subsequent struggle is called, and its outcome, are now a part of history and need no repeating here. Yet the full impact of war was only dawning on people gradually, as when for example a close friend or relative in the R.A.F. was killed. A kind of unreality reigned everywhere; one encounters this time and time again. On 28th July, Sir Henry Channon enjoyed "a gloriously hot day, and I lay in the sun and got beautifully burnt while planes zoomed on high." On 18th August Harold Nicolson had "a lovely day. I bathe in the morning . . . . While we are sitting outside, the air raid siren sounds. We remain where we are. Then comes the sound of aeroplanes and, looking up, we see thin streamers from the exhausts of the German 'planes." Then again on 26th August, also in the Nicolson diaries: "It seems so incredible as I sit here at my window, looking out on the fuchsias and the zinnias with yellow butterflies playing round each other, that in a few seconds above the trees I may see other butterflies circling in the air intent on murdering each other. One lives in the present." Channon felt that "we are living as people did during the French Revolution – every day is a document, every hour history."

London had been raided on 25th August, and during the next two weeks the pace was stepped up. By 7th September, when the first heavy daylight raid on London took place, and German transport barges were massed in the Channel ports and the tide and the weather were favourable, the British assumed that the invasion was under way. The code warning "Cromwell" went out at eight o'clock that evening. As church bells rang out across the Linconshire countryside to warn remote areas two Royal Engineers arrived at Lincoln Railway Station to blow it up before the enemy arrived. Luckily, the District Railway Superintendent insisted first on checking with his superiors and so discovered the real situation. The station was saved, but apparently some bridges were blown up before the word got around that it was all a false alarm.

Goering seems to have made a monumental tactical error in switching the emphasis of Luftwaffe attack from the airfields and control centres to London, just when the R.A.F. was beginning to find the strain on its resources almost intolerable. Between 24th August and 6th September alone British Fighter Command lost one quarter of its pilots and 466 Hurricanes and Spitfires. A chilling reality filled Churchill's words in the House of Commons on 20th August, that "Never in the field of human conflict was so much owed by so many to so few." Aircraft production workers were inclined to think that the boot was on the other foot: Churchill *should* have said, "Never . . . was so much owed by so few to so many" – referring of course to themselves. Others thought that the reference might be to the R.A.F. mess bills.

The bombing of London was, it seems, to have been the prelude to the actual German invasion. No wonder that people should have imagined that the invasion really had begun on 7th September. The switch of Goering's attack has been explained, in part at least, as reprisal for the bombing of Berlin by British aircraft early in September. More probably Hitler had already realized that he could no longer invade England that year, and so agreed to the bombing of London. After seeing the success of the German air attack on Rotterdam, Hitler doubtless hoped that similar treatment of London would bring the British to heel.

Goering's plan was to break civilian morale by concentrating bombing on the nation's capital. Initially the target was the Port of London docks, but soon the raids struck most areas of London. In any case, even concentration on the docks was bound to have repercussions on so large a built-up area as London. This is to say nothing of errors of aerial navigation, location of wrong target or similar eventualities, which must have scattered German bombs far and wide. From 7th September to 3rd November, then, London was raided every night. On 17th September Hitler postponed Operation Sea Lion either until the following spring or, as some think, indefinitely. The date of victory in the Battle of Britain is now celebrated as 15th September.

There has been a strong tendency to regard the Battle of Britain and the Blitz as two distinct phases of the war. Indeed, as far as the people of London were concerned, this was no doubt true. It is obvious now, however, that the two things overlapped, and were both directly related to the German invasion plans.

On 15th September the novelist J. B. Priestley said in one of his radio broadcasts – which were as popular as those of Churchill himself – that London was effectively thrown into the front line. This was how many people had always imagined it would be. The moment for which they had been bracing themselves had, at long last, arrived. Would this be truly their finest hour?

1. A Hideous Dream

Between the acting of a dreadful thing
And the first motion, all the interim is
Like a phantasma, or a hideous dream:
William Shakespeare *Julius Caesar*, ii, i.

"... This suspense is very trying ... Meanwhile, we are all blacking out, stuffing up cracks, laying in sand, *etc*. I think this is a good thing, as it gives people something they feel useful to do, and may actually diminish effects of raids, and therefore lessen fear and prevent collapse of nerves in crowded districts, and prevent a bad raid being a knock-out blow ... I feel we are living in a very bad dream, and still hope to wake before too late ...".

Rose Macaulay, 28th August, 1939.

Rose Macaulay's reference to the knock-out blow was right to the point. That was what was going to make this war different from any other that Britain had known. Of course, air attacks had taken place in the previous war but on nothing like the scale of those now feared. By scaling up the amount of damage caused by those attacks in 1914–18, official statisticians had estimated that the death and destruction in the next war would be of unimaginable proportions. As it turned out they were wrong, but one should bear this in mind before condemning Chamberlain's appeasement policy out of hand. In view of this prophecy of apocalyptic terror and catastrophe – many people referred to H. G. Wells's book *The Shape of Things to Come* (1933) – there was a very real sense in which a Prime Minister's first duty was to avoid plunging his country into such a war. Those with a wider vision saw that a confrontation with Hitler's Germany was bound to come sooner or later, and so greeted the declaration of war with some relief. If it had to come, the sooner the better. "Let's get on with it," was the general feeling.

In anticipation of this knock-out blow, then, Britain prepared her defence strategy. It seemed certain that the civilian population would be brought directly into the conflict. As the loss of life and property had been wildly overestimated, so had the probable effect of air attack on morale. Rose Macaulay may not have realized how crucial this was when she wrote about the "collapse of nerves in crowded districts." Of course, with both this and the question of the knock-out blow she may simply have adopted current official thinking on the matter, but they were both very real preoccupations at the time. In the case of public morale, the government could never have demanded what it eventually did of the nation if most people were not behind it. Hitler seemed genuinely surprised when Britain refused to sue for peace after the fall of France; some people in Britain thought at the time that such a move would have been highly sensible. But there was no panic; on very few occasions during the air raids on Britain was there any real sign of mass hysteria. The city of Coventry was, briefly, a case in point, but there were several reasons why the destruction of Coventry and other provincial centres was infinitely more serious than raids of similar intensity on London, as we shall see later.

In view of the estimated size of the disaster, one may well ask: why were some places so badly prepared to face the heavy air raids? Provincial cities do not seem to have learned much from the lesson of London; and within London itself the district of West Ham, for example, faced the Blitz notoriously unprepared. Government policy had been to make each local community and factory responsible for defence. Involvement with Air Raid Precaution duties was seen less as a contribution to the national defence, than as a direct service to the local community. The manifest flaw in this strategy was that a place with little community feeling would be poorly prepared, which was exactly the case of West Ham.

From early 1935, therefore, the urgency with which defence measures were put in hand was largely governed by force of opinion – from members of the government down to private individuals – as to whether or not war was inevitable, and if so, when it would be likely to happen. Undue pessimism would have alarmed people, created an atmosphere of tension and crisis, and disrupted national life. As became obvious in the worst days of the Blitz, it was the determination to keep going, to get things back to normal as soon as possible, that kept up morale. This was not in any tub-thumping, flag-waving way; but ordinary folk finding solace and comfort in the familiar humdrum of their daily lives. It was plain by the time of the Munich crisis, however, that a sense of national urgency now had to be instilled into war preparations.

By the end of August, 1939, much of the population accepted the fact that war was inevitable, that attack would come from the air, and that it would come almost at once. What was actually done in the way of defence?

The first feature may now seem hardly worth a mention, but for the people who lived through the war it represented something quite new in their lives. This was the air raid warning system, and in particular the penetrating wail of the sirens and the harmonious, comforting sound of the "all clear", which became familiar to most townspeople. At first the system had a chiefly operational, military role, in warning of attack. But by extending its use to civilian institutions and factories, and to the general public, more lives could be saved, because time was allowed to take shelter. The disruption of civilian life was kept to a minimum. When the Blitz was at its height, life sometimes seemed to be one long air raid. People lost track of whether a warning was in effect or not. Sometimes the warning did not sound before a raid began – as at Cardiff towards the end of June, 1940. But this was part of a definite policy to minimize the warnings so that loss of sleep and tension were reduced as far as possible.

The second feature of the defence system was the blackout. This duty rested fairly and squarely on the individual, whether as a private person, or as a manager of a factory, shop or offices. When the idea of blackout was first being debated, many larger firms hoped that it would be enough simply to switch off the lights when the air raid warning sounded. The recording company H.M.V., for example, had estimated that it would cost about £12,000 to fit its factory at Hayes, Middlesex, with blinds, then a considerable sum for one factory. The blackout was imposed very early in the war, and considering its limitations, people had amazing faith in it. At first not even flashlights were allowed in the streets at night, but as 1939 drew to a close and the nights became shorter, travelling became difficult and dangerous, especially for those who had to journey to and from work. By December about forty fatal accidents involving pedestrians took place each day, and so in January, 1940, the government eased the regulations. Apart from such accidents, there was the fear for women obliged to go out alone in the dark. By and large, however, criminal activity does not seem to have increased – certainly not in the early stages of the war.

Wardens were appointed to see that the blackout regulations were observed in the home. When violation of the regulations was made a punishable offence, this merely worsened already bad relations between Wardens and local people in some areas. The Wardens seemed to be police stooges, and were disliked. But such was the public's immense faith in the blackout that once their initial aversion to the Wardens had been overcome, they were often sterner towards offenders than the Wardens had ever been.

Camouflage was an anti-aircraft expedient of doubtful effect but of great psychological value. As was later revealed during air raids – especially during a full ("Bombers' ") moon – neither blackout nor camouflage was an adequate defence. Indeed, camouflage was almost useless once the enemy had located the target and lit up the area with incendiaries. The bombers simply followed in and released their loads. Smoke screens were also considered, and were used in some places. The idea seems to have appealed to Winston Churchill, who apparently toyed with the idea of enveloping large areas of the country in a permanent pall of smoke. Smoke screens served some useful purpose, but often hindered defenders as much as attackers.

Barrage balloons were another defence measure whose value was psychological rather than military. One children's book presented them as a race of benign aerial elephants. How successful they were is a moot point, but the fact that they reassured people was in itself worthwhile. Some mothers even returned from evacuation because there were no barrage balloons where they had been sent. The stirrup pump, which was inserted into a pail of water, held steady with the foot, and pumped up and down with a handle, had little defence value. By June, 1940, 86,000 of them were issued. A good water jet could be obtained by vigorously activating the pump, but they cannot have been much use if a blazing fire really took hold of a building. They were handy for watering the garden, however, and the author's family long used one after the war for this purpose.

The blackout extended not only to lighting of houses and streets, but to vehicles as well. Those on night guard in strange places knew how penetrating the car headlights could be. A single headlight might be visible many miles away and, owing to the movement of the car, even be mistaken for signalling. Yet, if the signal failed to make sense, where was the harm? But the crucial test was obviously whether the light could be seen by German aircraft; people had some rather odd ideas about what might be seen from the air. However, it was better to be safe than sorry, and such advice was all in a good cause. Drivers were asked to see that their masks were adjusted properly and that the headlight beams were not pointing upwards or emitting too much light. In an otherwise well-blacked out landscape a stream of car lights might give a vital clue along a road past an aerodrome, factory or power plant.

A special form of hooded headlight was designed for buses, motor cars and bicycles. Despite the many road accidents early in the blackout the faith of the people in the blackout overruled objections. One boy of seventeen, Michael Stapleton, whose unpublished memoirs are quoted elsewhere in these pages, spent the months of the Blitz in Hackney: "I was firmly instructed by a policeman on how to render my bicycle lamp serviceable. It was only to tell people that I was there, it wasn't to show me the way." He recalled how fierce people became about observing the blackout: "I remember that a fireman was covered in mud and grime and everything else, and was sitting on the kerb and lighting a cigarette, and he was screamed at by a hysterical woman. If ever a man deserved a cigarette, he did, but she wasn't thinking of that."

One of the best ways of securing the blackout would have been to have cut off electricity power supplies at source when raids began, but the government did not want to have to do this. However, faced with the general inconvenience caused by the blackout, they looked for other ways of alleviating the situation. One method was to extend summer time – daylight saving time – which was to have ended at the beginning of October, into the middle of November. As part of this relaxation of regulations, pedestrians were allowed to use flashlights in the streets, and special masked headlights were introduced for cars. But still the accidents happened. In 1940 the government introduced a summer time in February, which remained in force right up to the end of the year and throughout the war. In fact double summer time was introduced in May, 1941, and lasted until August. This expedient also continued for the duration of the war. As Michael Stapleton wrote: "You would get up in the morning, and as the year went on there was less and less daylight. With double British summer time, the hour of daylight you could expect was tacked onto the end of the day, so that you got a much longer ration of daylight at the end of the day, but you got none in the morning. I always went to work in the dark, and very often the raids were still going on. Somehow – not seriously – they always gave us the worst of it in the early part of the night, not the later part."

A third feature of defence – evacuation – will be dealt with in detail in the following chapter. From a defensive point of view it was not a success. The planning and conduct of the evacuation from London went extremely well, but social factors conspired to hinder the project much more than anyone had foreseen. In this respect evacuation was a failure. In areas outside London where it should have been introduced – and might have been done so with more success – it was not, thus entailing further loss of life.

Both evacuation and the fourth feature of defence – air raid shelters – were inspired directly by the government's policy of dispersal. As the term suggests, "dispersal" implied that both life, time, materials and labour would all be saved by avoiding massed populations which would present an easy target to the enemy. Nationally, this meant evacuation; but all those with essential war work to do were encouraged to stay, and for them adequate air raid shelters had to be provided. Those prophets of doom who advised the government believed that people would run to shelter as soon as the raids began, and be most reluctant to come out. Also, large shelters implied large concentrations of people, and the government's policy was dispersal. Accordingly, the onus of providing shelters was put on a local and individual level.

Feelings ran high when the government banned the use of the underground railway system as shelters and refused to build deep shelters on a large scale. People took the law into their own hands when the time came. They had sheltered in the tubes in the last war, and they would do so again. As to the lack of deep shelters, people obviously had less opportunity for decisive action. A group of underprivileged Londoners from Stepney did occupy the socially exclusive shelter of the Savoy Hotel by way of protest, but the incident received little publicity. The enormous cost weighted heavily against the government's undertaking a general programme of deep shelter building, but there was the dispersal policy to think of, too. In accordance with this policy, therefore, thousands of Anderson shelters (named after Sir John Anderson, the Home Secretary) were distributed free to the poor and at a modest charge to those who could afford it. Considering how simple and even fragile they were, the Anderson shelters were remarkably successful. They were made out of curved sheets of corrugated steel, which were then buried in the garden behind the house. They could hold from four to six people and protect them against most things, even a near miss.

Unfortunately, in the crowded streets of London's East End, where houses were often built back to back, there were no gardens in which to build Anderson shelters. There was little chance of giving up a room in the house for the purpose. Yet even if they could have had Anderson shelters, the East Enders would probably still have preferred the underground railways – where they had access to them – or the Victorian brick arches under the mainline railway tracks. Despite some appalling disasters, particularly under the railway arches, it was hard to convince people that they were better off elsewhere. They felt happier in a crowd, and some of the underground stations became very sociable places. People would stake out their claims, or send one member of the family to do so, and spread out their belongings. Bunks, installed later, met some opposition at first, since they reduced the amount of space available for sleepers, and restricted some of their activities.

At the height of the Blitz, Rose Macaulay had "a most odd journey home from Liverpool Street. The Central London tube was so crammed with thousands of shelterers that I couldn't get near the platforms at all, so pushed my way out again, with some difficulty, and took the Metropolitan. . . . It was a pathetic sight to see the shelter crowds in the tube, dossing down so uncomfortably for the night, sitting leaning against a wall, sometimes with a baby in a suit-case (open, of course). I suppose it is the warmth that brings them there instead of to the shelters . . .".

This warmth was human. The other alternatives were not very attractive. Brick shelters had been built in the streets, but these were not very substantial. They were really meant for passers-by who were caught unawares when a raid began. A positive danger existed in some: owing to an ambiguous government directive some authorities simply did not build them solidly enough, with the result that the concrete top was lifted clean off by a bomb blast and then came crashing down on the brick walls.

The long tunnel-like shelters in the public parks were repulsive to some. They, too, could be unsafe when lined with a certain concrete component which buckled under stress. *The Tatler*'s ubiquitous columnist Bridget Chetwynd finished off her "Social Round-about" of 4th September, 1940: "A grand policeman showed us round the trench shelters near the Serpentine. Very handsome they are, wriggling underground in an almost Greek key pattern. Nobody's any trouble, he says, except the officious ones." Despite the Alice-in-Wonderland evocation of Miss Chetwynd's description, shelter-going became a daily routine for many. Of course, some people adamantly refused ever to set foot inside a shelter and lived to tell the tale. Others took shelter and were killed. There was much to say for the maxim that you were often safe where you felt safe, and had tried it out. One unlucky exception was the Café de Paris, which advertised itself as the safest place in London. The raid of 8th March, 1941, proved the claim a disastrously hollow one.

Shelters are the subject of some interesting facts and figures. For example, by early November, 1940 – at the height of the Blitz – more than half the population of London never took shelter at all. As early as 23rd September of that year, two weeks after the Blitz began, Rose Macaulay wrote: "I am getting burying-phobia, result of having seen so many houses and blocks of flats reduced to piles of ruins from which the people can't be extracted in time to live, and feel I would rather sleep in the street, but know I mustn't do this . . . I think faith in tables is important. I think I shall put my mattress under one sometimes." A refinement of this idea was the Morrison shelter (after Herbert Morrison, Minister of Supply). This was basically a strengthened table with the sides filled in with wire netting. The author slept in one during a wartime visit to friends on the coast, and felt rather like a caged animal.

Of those who did go to shelters in London, more than half used Anderson shelters. Only two per cent went to tubes, and the rest to brick street shelters, large underground shelters and railway arches. Most tubes were safe – people had found this in the last war. But one or two nasty incidents did take place during raids. Balham Tube station was one of the worst, where the bomb damage was complicated by flooding. Another disaster occurred at Bank station, in which 111 people died. People were hurled off the platform by bomb blast, just when a train careered into the station, which had been plunged into pitch darkness by the explosion.

The fifth feature of defence was the manning of anti-aircraft guns and searchlights, coupled with the barrage balloons. In fact the defence of London depended primarily on the blackout, barrage balloons and anti-aircraft guns. But these "ack-ack" guns were little use against night attack, especially in the early days of the Blitz. Night fighters equipped with radar did not come into their own until early

1941. Early in 1938 all of Great Britain had only 100 anti-aircraft guns and 800 searchlights, yet more than 200 guns and 1,000 searchlights were needed for London alone. Furthermore, the anti-aircraft section seemed to have been plagued with the recruits rejected by all other sections. They were thus hopelessly ill-equipped to cope, until they were issued with radar two or three years later. At first, however, the booming of the guns had a great uplifting effect on morale. Londoners felt that they were fighting back, and that something positive was being done.

Finally, there were the various organizations of civilian personnel, without whom other defences would have been completely useless. Those ordinary men and women in the street functioned at local level, were volunteers (at first), and extremely varied in their degree of organization and strength. The various branches of A.R.P. worked in conjunction with local police forces and fire brigades. The operational unit of A.R.P. was the Wardens' Post. In theory there were ten such posts to every square mile, and from three to six wardens in each post. Naturally there was room for plenty of variation in practice. The wardens' task was not an easy one. In some places they were the subject of endless jokes until something actually happened. But soon the despised ranks of the A.F.S. and A.R.P., the stretcher bearers and ambulance people, came into their own. Very often they were working all day long and night as well. They were literally dropping on their feet. The wardens were to act as instructors to the population at large. They issued gas masks, made sure that the blackout was observed, and eventually reported "incidents", as and when they happened, to their control centre, usually in the local town hall. In this way suitable measures could be taken and ambulance, rescue unit, gas squad or fire services alerted. If any people experienced their finest hour at this time it was the wardens, rescue workers and firemen.

Some 200,000 wardens were appointed in London. Of these 16,000 were on a full-time basis and paid the princely salary of £3 a week. The rest had often done a full day's work before arriving for duty. Some were women. These were the people on the spot, who knew their districts and their people. Often they saved peoples' lives. The government booklet *Duties of Air Raid Wardens* (1938) contains a monumental simplification of the wardens' role: "In time of war, an air-raid warden should regard himself, first and foremost, as a member of the public chosen and trained to be a leader of his fellow citizens and, with them and for them, to do the right thing in an emergency." Eventually, this came true in a way that officialdom could never have hoped for.

The Home Guard, too, came to have an identity and standing that its early organization and personality belied. This was a quasi-military force of "civilian soldiers" recruited from those males who for one reason or another were not recruited by the armed forces proper. When H. V. Morton went to cover a secret meeting between Churchill and President Roosevelt in August, 1941, it is amusing to read that he took his Home Guard uniform along with him. He felt that civilian clothes were disliked by the Navy on such occasions, but not being in the forces he had no right to any other uniform. Morton speculated whether or not it was the first civil defence uniform to cross the Atlantic. When his Royal Marine servant unpacked his luggage he "withdrew my Home Guard uniform with an expression of gloom. 'Better send the trousers to the ship's tailor, sir,' he said. 'He'll get all this mud off and put a knife crease into them.' " The Marine was remarkably civil. The armed services did not have much respect for the Home Guard, nor, until the Blitz began, did the civilian population.

After the evacuation of Dunkirk Britain had only twenty-seven army divisions to defend the entire country. Three-quarters of her 1,000 anti-tank guns had been abandoned in France. Britain had only about 350 tanks of any kind, and shells were so scarce that it was not possible to fire practice shots. Plans were made for the police to resist German invaders; it is not clear who would have commanded them. Arms and ammunition were obtained, but were not issued to the men. One wonders what would have happened to the English police force if the German invasion had succeeded. Would they have been retained as an arm of the German occupation, or interned? Internment was easier in a small country like Denmark, than it would have been in Britain. Among German papers which came to light after the war were plans for the occupation of England; the entire male population between the ages of 17 and 45 was to have been interned, and despatched to the Continent. Concentration camps were actually prepared in occupied France for their reception, but the claim that the inmates were then to be sterilized has not been substantiated.

Could the British Resistance have done much in the event of invasion and occupation? David Lampe's fascinating book *The Last Ditch* reveals something of the resistance plans, but the known facts are comparatively few. King George vi had said that he would like to lead the British Resistance, although he could have been little more than a focal point for loyalty. Presumably he meant to show that he would go underground rather than collaborate with an occupying power. In case of emergency, twelve regional commissioners had been appointed in 1939, and if Britain had been invaded, or partially occupied, they would have had almost dictatorial powers. But there was no secrecy surrounding their appointment, which had been announced in the Press.

At the height of the Blitz, 1,500,000 men belonged to the Home Guard. Many other jobs had to be filled in Civil Defence services. These included wardens, rescue and stretcher parties, the people at control centres and messengers. Emergency ambulance workers and first-aid posts supplemented the casualty services. The Fire Service consisted of full- and part-time regulars and auxiliaries. The A.F.S. (Auxiliary Fire Service) was at first badly looked on and treated by the regulars. Auxiliary ambulance drivers were better treated. Ambulance work provided scope for women, particularly the more adventurous socialites. By December, 1940, the Fire Service accounted for another 1,500,000 men. In addition there were 250,000 full- and part-time policemen.

As the war drew more and more men away from their peacetime jobs it became clear that women would have to step into the breach. After all, they had done so in the previous war. This time, however, Britain actually conscripted women to war work – the first country to do so. At first, the trend to draw women into work was rather slow to develop. Between June, 1939, and June, 1940, there was an increase of fewer than 500,000 women in civilian employment. However, some 43,000 of them – all volunteers – had joined the three women's branches of the forces and the nursing services by 31st December, 1939. In June, 1940, Rose Macaulay wrote: "I have just been at the French Red Cross . . . and have probably got a job as an ambulance driver, to go off fairly soon if it comes off. No private cars can now get over. This would be driving ambulances for the French army at the front – interesting, quite, and I hope it comes off . . . I would rather, actually, drive an ambulance than work among refugees, as I have had more experience of it. I must now improve my mechanical knowledge, so as to be able to cope with all repairs if necessary. I will let you know any more I hear. I shall store my car again." She went on to refer to her possible demise: "If I *should* (improbably) get bumped off in the *mêlée*, I leave it to you. But that is most unlikely, I dare say I should be more likely to perish here."

Other women pursued less glamorous activities, but contributed as much to the war effort. For example, the normal staff of the Post Office in 1940 was about 330,000, of whom a third were women. By the end of 1941, 63,000 male Post Office workers had been conscripted. In 1940 the Army had been needed to help with the Christmas mail rush, so the Post Office tried to recruit some 60,000 women for Christmas, 1941, with the hope that many of them would stay on, as more people were certain to be conscripted in the future. Any woman aged sixteen or more was eligible. The ban on Christmas card production for 1942 alleviated the situation.

As the war progressed the manpower crisis became acute. Lord Beaverbrook's frenetic efforts as the new Minister of Aircraft Production kept the R.A.F. serviced and supplied, but it soon became clear that the immensely long hours he made his people work did not always lead to increased production. In June, 1940, women were limited to a sixty-hour week, and men the same in July. But the next year this figure was exceeded. A news item said: "Men should not, as a rule, work more than sixty hours a week, and women more than fifty-five, says a Government statement on the twenty-fifth report of the Select Committee on National Expenditure, issued last week. The Government urges managements to explain, where possible, the causes of production hold-ups, and stresses the necessity for a closer watch on wastage, absenteeism, and idle time."

With women playing a larger role than ever before, there were curious anomalies. In some parts of the country women taught men how to use their rifles; yet the Local Defence Volunteers, later renamed the Home Guard, refused to admit women. The Local Defence Volunteers had been formed by Anthony Eden on 14th May, 1940, in case of a German airborne invasion. Even before Eden had finished his announcement on the radio that evening, men were hurrying to their local police stations to join. It is doubtful how effective the Home Guard could have been against an invasion: it was trained to fight along conventional lines, but only guerrilla tactics could have succeeded had the Germans invaded England. A guerrilla force did exist, but all that was required of the Home Guard was that they should be "British subjects, between the ages of seventeen and sixty-five" and they were going to be "entrusted with certain vital duties for which reasonable fitness and a knowledge of firearms [was] necessary."

It seems odd that women were not catered for in the Local Defence Volunteers. Even if they were never to bear arms they could certainly have played full service-women's roles as telephonists, secretaries, drivers and administrators. Aroused by this insult, fifty women assembled in London and formed the Amazon Defence Corps. Amongst them was a keen riflewoman, Marjorie Foster, winner of the King's Prize at the Bisley rifle tournament in 1930. One of the Amazons' declared aims was "to encourage in all women the spirit to resist the invader by all means available."

Harold Nicolson was surprised to learn from Queen Elizabeth (the present Queen Mother) that she was having instruction each morning in how to fire a revolver. "Yes," she said. "I shall not go down like the others." Within a week of the beginning of the Blitz, Buckingham Palace was hit in a daylight raid. One of the bombs landed thirty yards from the room in which the King was talking and another destroyed the chapel. The Queen felt that she could now face the badly blitzed East End with a little more ease: "I'm glad we've been bombed", she was quoted as saying. "It makes me feel I can look the East End in the face." Rumour had it that when the King and Queen visited the East End they were booed. It would have been understandable. Although some of the first bombs also fell in the West End, it was the East End which took the first savage pounding of the Blitz. The West End represented money, security and privilege. The East End represented poverty, danger and inadequate defence resources. In fact royal visits soon became a source of comfort to people in the hard-hit areas, because they drew attention to their plight, even if they did no measurable practical good.

So Britain braced herself for war. Windows were boarded up, walls of sandbags were constructed and buildings were strengthened. In 1938, 275 million sandbags had been ordered, and the entire Scottish jute industry was involved. But it was realized that these would only be enough to protect government buildings and other essential sites such as A.R.P. centres. So in December, 1938, another 200 million bags were ordered from India to be delivered by August, 1939. By March of that year, Scotland and India were turning out 12 million bags a week. Even so, by the outbreak of war total orders had risen by a further 50 millions to 525 millions.

As 1939 drew on, more trenches were dug. Current projects were speeded up or extended, as was the supply of gas masks, which had first been issued in 1938 during the Munich crisis. Extensive use of gas was another gloomy forecast about German tactics which happily never came true, but it figured largely in the popular imagination as one of the terrors to come. The issue of gas masks meant that every adult Briton, for the first time in the country's history, went into a war with an item of personal defence. Just as the siren wails rapidly became a part of daily life, so did the pale brown cardboard containers which were carried everywhere. Many people gave up carrying them during the phoney war, despite the example set by officials who were seen with them all the time. But when the Germans advanced into Western Europe, the gas masks reappeared once more.

After Britain declared war on 22nd September, 1939, six weeks went by before Germany dropped the first bomb on British soil – in the remote Orkney Islands. More then eight months passed before the attack on the civilian population began. Within three weeks of the declaration of war, *The Times* said that the government had recruited too many people for A.R.P. work; that the restrictions on lighting and entertainment were too severe; and that in over-estimating the casualties, they had denied hospital facilities to those currently in need of them. Clearing the hospitals of all but serious cases had been an early government war measure.

The criticism mounted, much of it carefully expressed. As long as there was no war on the home front there was every reason to complain. But the government knew that if they lost their impetus now it would be doubly difficult to return even to the point reached when war was declared. In many respects Britain had been hopelessly unprepared to meet an all-out German attack at that time.

Neville Chamberlain, who was still Prime Minister, warned the country in a speech at the Mansion House in London on 9th January, 1940, that it "would have to face a phase of the war much grimmer than anything it had yet seen." His words cannot have had much effect. What the country had seen until now was hardly "grim".

But, in late August and early September, 1939, the trouble was the fine weather. As Rose Macaulay said, "Perfect weather: how we are wasting it . . ." It was hard to communicate any sense of urgency or impending doom on the long sunny days. Indeed even the following summer, when the Germans were daily drawing closer, many people commented on the heavy traffic on the roads at the Bank Holiday. Families of holidaymakers crowded the seaside resorts. Amid the sandcastles and deck chairs it was hard to believe that there was a war on.

2. A Nation on the Move

"There is hardly anything that shows the short-
sightedness or capriciousness of the imagination
more than travelling does. With change of
place we change our ideas; nay, our opinions and
feelings . . .".   William Hazlitt *On Going on a Journey*

A striking effect of the war was the amount of movement among the population
that it entailed. Men and women in the forces were moved from base to base, and
then overseas. For some this was a broadening experience they could never have
hoped for before. Michael Stapleton, who came to England as an immigrant with
his family from Ireland, had lived in London for nine years and had never had a
holiday. The day after the sinking of the *Bismarck* in May, 1941, he joined the
Merchant Navy and found himself bound for Africa, hitherto as remote to him as
the Land of Cockaigne.

But it was not only the fighting men and women who found themselves on the
move. In line with the government's policy of dispersal, a massive evacuation of
women and children was undertaken. At the upper end of the social scale, generally,
occurred another evacuation of those who had little reason for staying in danger
areas and had the money to take themselves away. This they did, often "for the
duration." A certain amount of ill-feeling was caused by this, but people who were
unable to contribute to the war effort were probably better out of things. The
columnist Cassandra (William Connor) of *The Daily Mirror* conducted a personal
feud against people he called "The Dermatologists" who saved their skins in 1940
by escaping to America. A discreet retirement in the country would have been the
better part of valour. Further population movement was caused as the manpower
crisis became more acute, and people were required to attend other places of work.
Finally, there were those rendered homeless by the coming of the bombs, and who
lost almost everything they possessed.

This enormous upheaval, which was quite unlike anything seen in the previous
war, was to have deep social consequences. Between the outbreak of war and the
end of 1945, some 60 million changes of address were recorded in a population of

38 millions. About 35 million of these changes were caused by people moving from one local government area to another; 14.5 million of these took place in 1940 and 1941. The population of the East End of London fell by more than half, until by June, 1943, London was to have only seventy-six per cent of its prewar population. Southampton fell to sixty-seven per cent. To add to this movement of people, some 30,000 people came from the European Continent to Britain, along with 29,000 from the Channel Islands – the only territory of the United Kingdom occupied by the Germans – and about 10,500 people from Gibraltar – all before the end of 1940.

Some two million people left London at the outbreak of war. In early 1941 *The Times* spoke of country hotels "filled with well-to-do refugees, who too often have fled from nothing. They sit and read and knit and eat and drink." The phenomenon was repeated on a smaller scale when the air raids really got under way. On 3rd September, 1939, Harold Nicolson had described a very different sort of evacuation: "There are many army lorries passing along the road and a few pathetic trucks evacuating East End refugees. In one of those there is an elderly woman who shakes her fist at us and shouts that it is all the fault of the rich. The Labour Party will be hard put to it to prevent this war degenerating into class warfare."

The novelist Rom Landau, who was in the R.A.F., was posted to Scotland, and was amazed by what he found there: ". . . The scene in front of the hotel, though no doubt quite customary here, was a surprise to me. Cars were arriving almost in a stream, to deposit men and women returning for dinner from golf courses, shooting parties, and fishing expeditions. Their gear in slick leather cases and bags was lifted from the cars by two dignified-looking porters and a page, less than five feet tall and dressed in a magnificent kilt. This was Scotland seen almost through the lens of Hollywood. The scene certainly did not suggest that a war was on and that a few hundred miles away, in England's southern skies, the battles in defence of Western civilization were being fought. When an hour later the hotel guests, without exception in evening dress, assembled for dinner, I, in my shabby Number Two uniform, felt an intruder from a world which was as commonplace to me as their elaborate clothes, shooting and cocktail parties must have been to them. Admittedly, most of them were either elderly or very young, and it was good to see that in a world going increasingly mad, there was still scope for a life that though not necessarily more civilized than that of those taking part in the general madness, was at any rate more pleasant. I was the only representative of the armed forces, and the inquisitive glances that met me in the dining-room showed plainly enough that the image of war, even symbolized as modestly as it was by my inconspicuous uniform, did not often intrude into that calmer world."

Some of those people were probably thinking that if he belonged to the armed forces, then he ought to be out shooting Germans. But, as Landau admitted, "The number of guests who at nine o'clock gathered round the wireless, and the tenseness with which the latest reports of the air battles in the south were listened to, showed that the gulf between the two worlds was far less real than first impressions might have induced one to believe."

Devon was another place of refuge. Bridget Chetwynd, who must have given the German propagandists as much ammunition for stirring up class hatred as anyone, reported in her "Social Round About" in *The Tatler* in September, 1940: "How they are doing in Devonshire . . . North Devon is packed, with people on leave from various jobs, and others who had the foresight to rent houses there for the duration, and have now evacuated themselves to enjoy a particularly fine summer. Among these Sir Pierce and Lady Lacy, whose own beautiful house, Ampton Hall, in Suffolk, is now in a danger zone. So they have rented a small house in Braunton from Mrs. Incledon-Webber, the local 'squiress', whose eldest son, Sam the cricket and rackets player, married their daughter, Angela. Geoffrey Toon, the young six-foot-two stage and film star, spent July and part of August at Cock Rock, a beautiful thatched-roof house with an exquisite garden, belonging to Miss Girvan. It is built almost on the beach at Croyde Bay, so he was able to surf and sun-bathe all day long, and get that rippling tan everyone fancies, before joining a battery at Portsmouth last week." Mr. Geoffrey Toon at least joined his battery at Portsmouth, but Miss Chetwynd's gay badinage can hardly have been calculated to improve class relationships. This was the last issue of *The Tatler* before the Blitz was unleashed on London.

As to the other form of evacuation – the official variety – the first move had simply been to get the children out of London. But as German armies advanced into Western Europe in May, 1940, the south and east coasts of England suddenly became danger areas, and it was imperative for the government to move away the London children who had been evacuated there. Next, the local children had to be moved to safety to South Wales and the Midlands. Evacuation was not compulsory, but the closing of the state schools induced people to leave.

After this the government called for evacuation of the London and Thames area, of the north-east coast, and of those parts of the south coast unaffected by the first of these new measures. Since the first wave of evacuation had oozed away, the response to this renewed call to evacuation was, not surprisingly, meagre. But when the bombing began, the railway stations were once more packed with evacuees making for places of sanctuary.

A scheme was formulated to send children to safety abroad. By mid-August over 19,000 applications had been approved by the new Children's Overseas Reception Board. Ninety-nine per cent of these children were attending state or state-aided schools. As before, the rich made their own arrangements. On 24th June, 1940, Sir Henry Channon recorded: "I was called at 7, dressed and ate nervously; at 8.15 we set out for Euston. Honor and I had the child between us; he was gay and interested. At the station there was a queue of Rolls-Royces and liveried servants and mountains of trunks. It seemed that everyone we knew was there on the very crowded platform . . . . We led our child to his compartment, and clung hungrily to him until the whistle blew and then after a feverish hug and kiss, we left him . . .". Not all children were able to depart in such style, and the sinking of the liner *City of Benares* on 17th September abruptly ended official arrangements to evacuate children overseas.

At the beginning of the war 1,500,000 mothers and children were successfully evacuated from London; by the end of 1939 two-thirds of them had come back. By May, 1940, as few as 250,000 children remained in their places of refuge.

That evacuation failed there is no doubt, although the operation had been well planned. But some evacuees did settle permanently in their new homes. In the author's village – then the centre of a close-knit farming community between the Durham coalfield and industrial Teesside – one of the girls evacuated from Teesside became so attached to her adopted family that she never returned home; she continued to live with her foster parents long after the war.

Why did evacuation fail? Harold Nicolson noted in his diary: "The House [of Commons] is mainly concerned with the evacuation of children. It seems that where children have been evacuated along with their school teachers everything has gone well. But when mothers have come, there has been trouble. Many of the children are verminous and have disgusting habits. This horrifies the cottagers upon whom they have been billeted. Moreover, the mothers refuse to help, grumble dreadfully, and are pathetically homesick and bored. Many of them have drifted back to London. Much ill feeling has been caused. But the interesting thing is that this feeling is not between the rich and the poor but between the urban and the rural poor. This is a perplexing social event . . . the effect will be to demonstrate to people how deplorable is the standard of life and civilization among the urban proletariat."

It seems that the children had been taken away at the end of the summer holiday, and so were more verminous than they would have been in term time. In the words of the official report, *On the State of the Public Health during Six Years of War*: "It is not surprising that, in this general movement of population, misfits occurred, and that concern was expressed at the standards of cleanliness and conduct found in many of the evacuees. In some districts it was found necessary to cleanse children several times during the course of a year. The root cause of these conditions lies in the home of the child. Slum clearance has not yet gone far enough. Low standards of living persist and the lessons taught in the school and clinic sometimes fail to reach the older generation."

Rose Macaulay found that "the evacuated mothers are many of them complaining bitterly about country life – no gas or electricity often, coal fires, hard beds, too few shops, *etc.* – and their hosts and hostesses of course resent this. Some of them will probably return to London and face the bombs, I expect."

She was right. But this was early September, 1939, and no bombs would come for a year. The problem continued to concern her: "A sensible talk from some woman about evacuees the other day, I thought. She advised house-holders to learn to put up with a little dirt, and evacuees to learn to put up with a little soap and water. Very sound. Country cottages can never have been thought so clean before, I should think! It seems they are shocked at insects and dirty habits in a way that shows they never heard of them before."

The author remembers the shock and horror when it was found that children in his village had caught head lice from evacuees. A definite moral stigma was attached to it. To have lice was comparable with receiving divine retribution. It was, after all, one of the plagues visited on the Egyptians. There were still, at that time, very real differences between townspeople and country folk. In September, 1940, Cecil King made a bonfire for his wife's thirty-five evacuees; the children had never seen a bonfire before. When it was fairly blazing they asked him, "When are you going to put the bombs on?"

Evacuation put enormous strains on local resources. Yet had there been enough goodwill much more could have been done to make it work. One cannot pigeon-hole the problem as a direct confrontation between urban and rural poor; it was more subtle than that. The author remembers toward the end of the war, being one of several village children trying to decide which families would be forced to take evacuees. One took a rather vicious delight in revealing that Mrs. So-and-so had one or two empty rooms, and so would have to take some. Children being what they are, most of this must have come directly from their parents; the evacuees were pawns in an elaborate chessgame of retaliation for some past, but well remembered, transgression. The question of how well an evacuee would suit a particular home did not arise.

But when the country people really set their minds to catering for the boys in uniform, they could almost produce miracles. The vicar of a rural parish in north-west England was delighted at the response to a request for a social club for the nearby military camp. Almost overnight a vacant cottage in the village was donated, and furniture, crockery and a radio materialized. Equally, these amenities could vanish overnight when the soldiers were posted, and a batch of conscientious objectors was brought in. The authorities, with instinctive flair for creating the most ill-feeling, arranged for the "conchies" to be brought from the nearest railway station in coaches, whereas the military had gone on foot.

Britain's record on conscientious objectors in the two world wars is not one to be proud of. There was, of course, the enlightened liberal approach of Rose Macaulay: "I know a pacifist who makes it his war work to go round the tubes spraying the shelterers with disinfectant in the night – very brave . . .". She did not explain whether the man should be admired for braving the bombs or braving the shelterers. One self-appointed guardian of the nation's conscience, *The Sunday Pictorial*, demanded in the summer of 1940 that all pacifists should be locked behind barbed wire. An absurdly high regard was held for the man in uniform. Rom Landau observed this when he returned to London during the Battle of Britain: "The man in the street and the press alike referred to the R.A.F. with a fervour which seemed as un-English as it was personal. You might have thought that everyone in London had a son or brother among the Fighter boys. As I soon discovered, for a wearer of the grey-blue uniform with wings on the breast, situations often arose that were embarrassing. Wherever I went, I found people glancing at my uniform and my air-gunner's badge with an expression of affection. . . . In several shops in which I made purchases my 'Good-bye' was met with a 'Good-luck' and one or two shop assistants insisted on shaking hands with me, something unique in all my previous experience."

This was, however, one of the less remarkable aspects of the phenomenon. At the other end of the scale it made quite ordinary home-loving women suddenly feel called upon to bestow their favours on almost any man in uniform. A man in uniform was virtually a hero, irrespective of whether he had seen a single action. But a declared pacifist or conscientious objector was seen as less than human; it was of no interest that he might be doing heroic work in hospitals or with ambulances; or filthy jobs which no one else wanted to do, sometimes in highly dangerous conditions, or that many men in "essential" employment were scandalously idle.

Of course, parents and wives who lost soldier sons and husbands, and fighting men who saw comrades fall at their side, were bound to feel bitter against those who, in their eyes, ought to have taken their dear ones' places. Less jingoism was evident in World War Two than there had been previously, but even now it is hard for many people to reconcile what they know to be the reality of war with the sentimental attitude of mind summed up, for example, in Rupert Brooke's poem *The Soldier*. One would like to think that things have changed. Living under the shadow of the atomic bomb has probably helped to put things in perspective.

Parallel with the rather hysterical animosity to conscientious objectors was that displayed towards aliens. Many quite harmless people (many of them brilliant artists and scientists) who had fled Nazi persecution now found themselves

C

interned on the Isle of Man. After the initial shock, some of them organized themselves into a "university" – a university which surely must have had one of the finest teaching staffs anywhere in the world at the time. Through the accounts we have, endorsed by several of the internees, the officers in whose charge they found themselves were mostly kind and considerate.

Not all those interned were treated with the same degree of severity. Some were treated so well that the local people were up in arms. Emergency Regulation 18b, under which aliens were interned, seems to have been a two-edged sword. The German Consul-General in Iceland was held there until the British Ambassador in Brussels was released. German radio claimed that the Consul had been consigned to the Tower of London and treated like a criminal. In fact he and his family and staff – according to the British Press – occupied a fifteen-bedroomed mansion just outside Douglas on the Isle of Man, and, in the words of a local inhabitant, "lived like lords." Lively local speculation took place as to where their cigarettes came from.

It is amazing how many people moved around – considering the difficulties of travel – when they were not on official business. At the end of May, 1940, to compound the difficulties, the government ordered that "no person shall display or cause or permit to be displayed any sign which furnishes any indication of the name of, or the situation or the direction of, or the distance to any place." In anticipation of imminent invasion, when – it was supposed – German parachutists would drop from the skies disguised as nuns or miners, it was decided to confuse the enemy, quite apart from the great British public, by removing all signposts and street names. In towns these were not replaced until the autumn of 1942, and in rural areas until the middle of 1943. But truck drivers in military convoys discovered that they could often navigate by manhole covers or drain lids, which were usually inscribed with the name of the nearest town. It was easier still if a telephone kiosk was at hand. For some reason it was overlooked that kiosks give their precise location neatly on a label inside.

But the less astute were less lucky, as Rose Macaulay wrote to her sister: "I hear hundreds of walkers, cyclists and motorists are now lost in the countryside, all sign-posts and names of villages taken down, and the public advised to give no information to enquirers, which seems cruel. I feel there should be some shibboleth. Mind you stop *at once* if a man with a gun tells you to, as they now have leave to shoot those who don't, and a lot of untrained men are wandering about with rifles looking for parachuters, who are often dressed as nurses. So do be careful. Dear me, what a fantastic world we have come to inhabit!"

The proprietress of one rural café mislaid a map of the locality, which had been lying around on her premises when a couple of military policemen were there.

Suddenly, after casually mentioning her loss to an officer, she found herself attending an identity parade of a whole squad of military policemen. Since presumably the officer did not suspect his own men of being spies, one can only assume that he was taking great pains to keep relations with the local inhabitants on a good footing.

On railway stations, place names had to be no more than three inches high, and within twenty miles of the east and south coasts, non-existent. Buses and trams displayed no destinations. *The Tatler* had some very unfunny things to say about the situation in railway stations. Apparently an official document had suggested that "the least costly method to the railway companies would be to arrange that the name of the station should be shouted distinctly by the railway staff." But as the report was well aware, "at some country stations the local dialect might leave the ordinary traveller in the dark, while standard English might fog the local inhabitant." This gave the correspondent of *The Tatler* positive *frissons* of righteous indignation. *Sabretache*, the correspondent in question, went on: "The public is very long-suffering, and it does not ask for much: it might not even go so far as to clamour for lessons in elocution and voice production for porters, but I think it has a right to demand that when a train stops at Harrow, the local announcer should not so pronounce that word as to make it sound exactly like Eton. I think that it is high time that the o.e. [Old Etonian] and o.h. [Old Harrovian] associations joined in a joint vigorous protest." Had this terrible thing already happened to *Sabretache*, or is it possible that he was attempting a joke?

To be fair to the magazine, however, it was also concerned with the more practical aspects of travel in difficult circumstances, even if they were of a slightly esoteric nature: "These night watches put a big strain on a small car, many of which are doing good work on transporting the Home Guard to their posts along deeply rutted farm tracks, up rocky hillsides and even over open country. The modern 'eight' or 'ten' was never designed to take four jolly farmers, their great-coats, gumboots and rifles to these outlandish places. Nor is a bunch of rifles one of the most convenient war props one can carry in a car. Also it's destructive for the upholstery unless wrapped in a rug or tarpaulin. For which reason I'd like to hear of some kind of clip or support that would allow of four rifles being carried upright in a car instead of sprawling over the seats. Unfortunately the average small car body is not wide enough to enable the rifles to be laid across the floor." If nothing else was achieved, those readers of *The Tatler* who mounted guard as local defence volunteers in remote rural places could exercise their ingenuity in devising a clip or support.

Petrol rationing kept a certain amount of traffic off the roads, particularly private cars, though initially a number of people were reluctant to observe the interests of the nation and continued driving as they had done before. But this was September, 1939. One trusts that the picture would have been different in 1940. Rose Macaulay wrote: "I hope to come on Wed: afternoon – by road, as we have a week's respite before petrol rations. It was a great sight last Friday night to see the cars queuing up for miles round each garage to fill up before midnight. Lots of them were also filling containers, which was illegal as well as selfish. And then after all it was put off . . .".

During bank holidays, however, particularly during the summer of 1940, one would hardly have thought Britain was at war. Thousands of people took to the roads and flocked to the beaches. The Blitz altered that, coupled with the ever-present threat of invasion. By the end of 1941 when the threat had receded, it was again possible to visit coastal resorts. But private cars were not allowed near them so one either had to go by train or leave one's car at a certain point and continue the journey by bus.

The war severely strained the country's railway system and many passenger services had to be axed as men and materials were moved around. Further cuts had to be made towards the end of 1941. There were twenty-five per cent fewer main line services than in peace time, but during 1941 the railways ran more than 30,000 special military trains and over 8,500 special coal trains. In fact coal traffic during the winter of 1941–42 was running at an estimated 250,000 tons more than during the previous winter, which had been one of the coldest so far in the century. Although passenger services were hit special arrangements were made to ensure that war workers were not hampered in getting to and from work. Even so a journey scheduled to take less than an hour to or from London might take several hours, and trains could set off for one station and arrive somewhere quite different. That so many managed to attend work so often in these circumstances was remarkable.

In the streets of London one could expect literally anything during the Blitz. When Balham underground railway station was hit in a raid, a bus driver stopped his vehicle and took shelter. When he came back his bus had gone, and he assumed that someone had moved it for him. As he got closer, however, he saw what had really happened; his bus had fallen straight into a huge hole in the road.

Michael Stapleton recalls that there was a progressive dislocation of traffic as the Blitz got under way: "The buses and trolley-buses, and such trams as remained – and there were a few, even then – could sometimes be completely halted. With buses it was different, because they could sometimes be switched off the route, then back onto it, but a trolley-bus couldn't. If an air raid had brought down the overhead wires they were stranded like whales and they could do nothing. A tram could never get over a hole in the road, it just stopped and came back again."

Things continued to deteriorate: "It was getting more difficult to get to work because as the raids increased in regularity, and areas that hadn't been affected were being affected, the main roads would suddenly stop dead because there was a great big hole in the middle of them or because a high building had been hit and had simply fallen across the road. You just had to get out and trample around it, and hope that you could pick up transport at a point farther on."

Londoners became used to this sort of thing, and it has probably stood them in good stead ever since. They bear delays and interruptions to commuter services with remarkable fortitude. Of course, as London is made up of many individual boroughs and once-rural villages, there are many self-contained areas of community life. Sometimes there are very practical reasons for this, for example bad transport services, but some areas, such as Marylebone High Street, are very close to the heart of London, yet still preserve a separate identity. Although a great deal of movement takes place within the London region, many people do not move much at all. This was true of the war period, and the war tended to emphasize it. So although a great many people moved around, those who generally moved little tended to move even less.

This explains why, despite the fact that a great part of the population was on the move, there was remarkably little communication between people about the latest developments in the war, except where, for example, there was a tradition of regular family correspondence. The Press and the radio had to censor themselves and be censored. It soon became obvious to people that they were being told far less than the whole truth in both the newspapers and on the radio. The question of communications will be dealt with in more detail in Chapter Four, but it helps to explain why Rom Landau found that there were almost "two nations" in England in 1940. "London far more than the North reflected the country's reactions to the achievements of the R.A.F. Whereas the North was separated from the southern scenes of air warfare by several hundred miles and, in consequence, seemed hardly aware of what the R.A.F. was doing, in London people spoke of little else but the daily air battles over the south coast and the Channel. Every letter I received from London, every London newspaper, confirmed this. The amazing feats of our fighter boys evoked among Londoners a wave of exaltation that in its intensity at times appeared almost religious. It was as if London dimly felt that the achievements of our fighters were something more even than appeared on the surface." They were certainly right.

Had television been nationwide and still on the air, there probably would have been a more acute sense of national involvement, assuming the government did not censor everything. This may have helped the provincial centres who were apparently taken totally unawares by the bombs. If they could have seen the effects of the raids, their own plight may have seemed less grave. Of course the very fact of witnessing such events in the comfort of a living-room might have rendered people immune to death and destruction, much as we have now seemed to become immune to war and natural disasters when shown on our television screens. At that time, however, the effect might well have been the converse – broken morale. Furthermore, the Germans would have been able to see just how much damage they had done. As it was, in Churchill's estimation, popular ignorance was probably bliss, and it was almost certainly folly to be wise.

There was, of course, more to the question than that. As late as 11th June, 1941, in a House of Commons debate, Mr. H. Willink, who had been appointed Special Commissioner for the homeless people of London, was able to say, "Nobody in my office, or myself, has ever been asked for any general information on the way London attempted to deal with this problem [of post-raid services] by any local authority in England, Scotland or Ireland." This was particularly odd in the case of Scotland. Clydebank had had a very bad experience of air raids, and regional officers from Scotland had looked into the problems that had been experienced by London in the raids as early as September, 1940 – in other words within two or three weeks of the start of the Blitz. Moreover the Scottish Department of Health had put out a thirty-two page guide on 12th December, 1940, which was inspired principally by London's experience.

In the face of adversity each town or city seemed to assert its independence fiercely, and was determined to bear its agony alone. In the event they often needed outside help when things were desperate. The government's policy may have encouraged this parochial outlook, or perhaps, in spite of so much population movement, people looked first to their home territory as a matter of instinct. Or again, with the whole nation apparently in a state of upheaval, it was only possible to think in terms of one's own town. The evidence would seem to point to the first explanation, however. The government's decision to put responsibility at local authority level pervaded the whole field of air raid precautions and post-raid services in the first phase of the war.

3. A Consumer Society at War

"Zoning now restricts Mars to the Southern
Counties. So here's hoping for quick victory – and
plenty of Mars for everyone – everywhere."
Wartime advertisement for confectionery

Whether Napoleon was right or wrong when he described the English as a nation of shopkeepers, World War Two showed how advanced Britain was as a consumer society, and how much she depended on trade and maritime traffic to keep that society consuming. Officially she was fighting to save herself – and Western civilization into the bargain – and certainly that was a much more inspiring motive than trade in those troubled times.

In economic terms, however, Britain's victory was a Pyrrhic one indeed. If any one visual image put this across, it was surely the famous cartoon by Zec which appeared in *The Daily Mirror* on 6th March, 1942 – all the more remarkable because it was produced then – showing an exhausted sailor clutching a raft in the midst of an empty sea. The caption ran: " 'The price of petrol has been increased by one penny.' – Official." The publishers maintained that the cartoon (which was one of a series) was meant to remind the public that black marketeers were hampering the nation's war effort, and were squandering materials such as petrol for which seamen were drowning. The government had increased the price of petrol by a penny, but was that really going to make any difference? Many took the cartoon in this sense. Others detected crueller implications, and the fact that it was susceptible of several interpretations was, in a sense, a testimony to the genius of the cartoonist. The cartoon still stands as a powerful statement about the realities of war in the twentieth century.

The official publication *On the State of the Public Health during the War* puts the matter fairly succinctly – though in the specific context of food – and in so doing indicates the substance of this chapter: "It had always been realized that though the war could be won only by the fighting forces, it might well be lost on the food front and that one of the enemy's military objectives would be, as in the last war, the starvation of these islands. . . . The need to economize in food and in the labour required for its preparation and transport made it necessary to place many restrictions on the traditional methods of trade and competition. . . . The problem of feeding the nation was threefold. First to reduce calls on shipping to a minimum, in order to free as many ships as possible for the transport of men and munitions; secondly, to arrange for the equitable distribution of such food as was available in quantities sufficient to assure an adequate diet for all, whatever their income might be (although in peacetime this was never so); and thirdly, to pay special attention to those on whom the future of the nation depended."

At the beginning of the war stocks of most goods were sufficient, and rationing helped maintain this situation. But the situation gradually deteriorated and in October, 1941, the government was forced to adopt new measures. In an attempt to stop national resources being wasted, and to help shopkeepers make a reasonable living in the face of dwindling turnover, no new shops were to be opened without a Board of Trade licence; existing shops were not allowed to sell goods which they had not sold before. Food shops were exempted from this order, however. Permission for new shops was to be granted only in special cases – where for example an area was badly served for essential goods, or where a shopkeeper had been bombed out and wished to resume business near his old premises. A term of imprisonment for up to three months or a fine of up to £100 or both, were the penalties for contravening the regulation. In human terms things did not happen quite as the government wanted – certainly not at first. For one thing rationing was slow to take effect. Of summer, 1940, Michael Stapleton could say: "rationing had been introduced, but even so, there was no real shortage. There was no shortage of meat, for one thing, and it's in a thing like that that you really begin to feel there's a war on."

But the phrase, "Don't you know there's a war on!" – never put as a question – came to mean more as the Blitz got under way: "Smithfield [the London meat market] went on, most of the big markets went on as best they could. At times it came to a complete standstill, and there was nothing. But it was just about that time, for instance, that meat rationing really began to bite. You got your ration and that was all you got. This hadn't happened before. There was always some more of something. There were things which weren't rationed, and I remember my boss used to experiment with different ways of making sausages with less and less meat. He'd put vegetables in them. Well it was an old joke that most sausage was bread anyway. But he was rather clever with his seasoning and people rather liked them. If the ration had been half-a-crown, you might get three-and-six, but even that began to dwindle and you were right down to what you could get, what you were legally entitled to, and no more. Things like offal were still off the ration, but there wasn't much of it, and as soon as any came in it was immediately spotted and bought up at once."

There was a certain Wonderland quality about rationing since there were no restrictions in restaurants. William Connor (Cassandra) of *The Daily Mirror*, with his usual flair for controversy, conducted a personal survey of restaurants called a "Gutskrieg", to reveal some of the excesses then prevalent. This was one more source of irritation in the shaky relations between a highly sensitive Churchill and *The Daily Mirror*. After much correspondence and a lengthy interview, Cecil King went far toward reassuring Churchill that the newspaper was on his side. At times, Churchill might well have wondered how true this was.

Although the *Mirror* advocated action, Cecil King only seems to have been capable of resignedly noting the situation. At the beginning of March, 1941, for example, one reads in his diary: "The shops are certainly less well stocked with goods of all kinds, but life remains very much pre-war. I do not yet discern any really strenuous war effort. It is still all very genial, half-hearted, and happy-go-lucky. The meat ration is small; the meat is never hung properly and so it is usually tough; fish is scarce and dear and not very fresh; eggs are hard to come by and cheese is almost unobtainable. But though this sounds bad, and though it may seriously affect the poorest classes, I would not say that we at home are suffering any noticeable inconvenience, let alone hardship."

In the same month – March, 1941 – it was still possible to see people dressing for dinner and dancing in Torquay when Plymouth was being bombarded by the Luftwaffe less than thirty miles away. On the menu for breakfast was a choice of fish, eggs or brisket of beef, with toast, porridge and jam. Dinner was soup or cocktail, ham, poultry, pudding and coffee, and all for 7s. 6d. (37½p). Obviously conditions were different outside London, and everywhere they were to get worse, but in London they got much worse. When the author was first taken to London one Easter towards the end of the war a waitress in the hotel produced a hot-cross bun as if it were a pot of caviar. One had to queue for hours at the restaurant at London Zoo for a plate of nauseous "bubble-and-squeak", a mixture of cabbage and potatoes fried up with dried egg. We cut short our holiday. The Lake District, where we travelled next, was almost another country, even another world, in comparison.

Rationing had become, along with the queue, part of wartime life. Ration books had been printed in 1938, but were not issued until the end of September, 1939, and the full force of rationing did not appear until 1942. People had to register with a retailer before 23rd November, 1939. On 28th November the government announced that rationing would begin on 8th January. Four ounces of bacon or ham (a nice distinction) and four ounces of butter were allocated to each person, and the sugar ration was fixed at twelve ounces per week. At the end of January the bacon ration was doubled; oddly, this was more than the average individual had consumed before the war. On 11th March meat was rationed to 1s. 10d. (9p)-worth per person over the age of six per week. For children under six the ration was 11d. (4½p) worth.

In mid-1940 a committee of experts was formed to advise the government on foodstuffs. The committee produced a "basic diet". It decided that a person could live on a daily intake of twelve ounces of bread, sixteen ounces of potatoes, two ounces of oatmeal, one ounce of fat, six ounces of vegetables and six-tenths of a pint of milk – with more of the same items listed, or augmented with cheese, pulses, meat, fish, sugar, eggs and dried fruit. In May the sugar ration was cut back to eight ounces, and in June bacon went back to four ounces. To our calorie-conscious age, so much starch is a daunting proposition. The high point of the endeavours of those who juggled with the nation's nutrition was perhaps the emergence of the National Loaf. It was about as unattractive as it sounds. In all fairness to them, however, the nation survived.

The situation was slightly helped by propaganda campaigns to grow more. But more definite aid came when, in response to Churchill's request to America in February, 1941, to "Give us the tools and we will finish the job," the Lend-Lease bill became law in March of that year. It was not directly strategically effective, since many of the arms were still paid for in dollars, but towards the end of May supplies of dried egg, evaporated milk, bacon, cheese, lard and tinned meat began to reach Britain. These supplies accounted for one-fifteenth of all food arriving in Britain in 1941. In the early months of the year the total was only two-thirds of the amount imported before the war. Official estimates had been for 35 million tons over the course of the year. By spring this was reduced to 31 millions and in the event only 30.5 million tons got through.

The meat ration went up to 2s. 2d. (11p) per week in the last quarter of 1940, but in January of the next year it had to be slashed to 1s. 2d. (6p) where it stayed. The legal position with meat was complicated by the fact that, because of the war, it had become Crown property, and so was no longer subject to inspection by local authorities. This made the whole problem of distribution worse than it need have been.

On an annual average, wholesale prices rose by about fifty per cent between 1939 and 1941. Consumer goods became more and more scarce. There were long queues and rising prices and the black market. The price of some commodities in short supply was fixed, but without rationing this simply meant that they were either stockpiled by those with cash, or else kept by shopkeepers "under the counter" for favoured customers. In December, 1940, food prices for a wide range of commodities were frozen; even more tended to disappear from view.

In March, 1941, jam, syrup and treacle, along with margarine, were put on a new basis of a minimum of eight ounces monthly, but in July this was revised to a ration of a pound, without any minimum or maximum. (It should be borne in mind that in many city slums, bread and margarine were the staple diet of the family.) In May cheese was put on ration for the first time, at the rate of one ounce per week. A notice which appeared in the Press late in November, 1941 must have drawn a wide variety of reactions. The Food Ministry announced that roadmen employed by rural councils were to be eligible for the special cheese ration of eight ounces per week. In June, the distribution of eggs was controlled, though there was no actual rationing. As far as the consumer was concerned, however, this amounted to the same thing. Only the allocation system varied according to certain priorities. Rose Macaulay wrote to her sister early in September: "Thank you both *so* much for the three eggs. If I had known there were three I wouldn't have taken them all, you can have none left, but it is wonderful to see three eggs together, almost a miracle; *one* is remarkable. I daren't cook one yet, as it is better not to turn the gas on while bombs are about, I believe, but later in the night, if these pests should recede, I shall."

The advent of food rationing had some odd social side affects. Towards the end of the war, when being sent away for a few days to friends – even very close friends of the family – the author was always provided with some rashers of bacon, an egg or two, and occasionally some butter. The rations were handed over with solemnity on arrival. The mother of one fairly large family could not understand why one of her daughters never seemed to worry at the shortage of butter and margarine, until she caught her late one evening equipped with a thin knife paring off the portions of the other members of the family. It became unpatriotic to use jam dishes: the Minister advised housewives that the spooning of jam out of jars and into dishes, and then back again into the jar, wasted the jam.

In her novel *The Heat of the Day*, Elizabeth Bowen builds an entire passage around the problem of rationing and its effects:

" 'Dear me,' said Robert, having received his [slice of bread], Mrs. Rodney and I forgot about bringing our own butter.' This served to draw Stella's attention to the butter arrangements: each one of the family had his or her own ration placed before his or her own plate in a differently coloured china shell. Today was the delusive opening of the rationing week; the results of intemperance, as the week drew on, would be to be judged. Stella's solitary Londoner's footloose habits of living, in and out of restaurants, had kept from her many of the realities of the home front: for some reason, the sight of the coloured shells did more than anything so far to make her feel seedy, shady; though she could not but admire the arrangement as being at once fanciful, frank and fair. She said hurriedly that she did not eat tea."

In such circumstances, the faking of ration books – for example by trying to erase cancellations in order to get a second ration – became for some a regular procedure. Bleach was one of the substances used, although on the pinkish-buff page it simply drew attention to itself, and was easily detected. The plight of larger families with several growing children to feed was hard. Those with the least resources tended to be hardest hit. It was the old syndrome of the poverty of the poor. No black market for them. It was a great help if one had friends or relatives in the country, who would send homegrown fruit and vegetables. Even at the height of the Blitz food parcels managed to penetrate the postal services, and made a welcome addition to a dull diet. In England, however, city dwellers tend to have abandoned their rural connections much sooner than, for example, in France, where almost everybody seems to know someone or have relatives in the country, even today.

Women became adept at improvising and "making do". The author's family had always lived in the country, and during the war experienced no great hardships. American or Canadian dried egg reached us, but we never seemed to lack fresh eggs. We did not see a banana until the end of the war, and then had little liking for them. Dried banana was revolting. A box of Canadian apples arrived at our home near Christmas one year. The apples were red and shiny, and sweet and juicy, and each one was individually wrapped in purplish-blue paper, as exotic in its way as a box of wartime Swiss chocolates. Few oranges were to be had, but this was not a special cause of concern. Our grandmother had heard that the Germans were planting bombs in oranges to kill innocent children.

A turkey was usually to be had at Christmas, although to obtain the bird invariably meant that someone had to know someone, or else wait for hours in a queue. We seemed to have a particularly large turkey one year. The author was, however, terrified to go into the larder where it hung before being plucked. It seemed colossal. Then there was a hair-raising journey home with a lobster as a companion on the back seat of the car. It seemed to be still alive, because every time we went around a right-hand corner this scarlet monster edged a little closer. It had been a traumatic day altogether.

The official report on the food situation during the war has a kind of detached objectivity which is quite unrelated to how people actually lived: "Articles which were not in short supply were left unrationed, though as the war went on, most of them became subject to price control. As demand increased the price of unrationed foods tended to rise, for example fish and some vegetables rose to excessive prices until control was exercised. A few articles, such as game and shell-fish, which were always so scarce that a rationing system could not be worked, were left uncontrolled, and with these alone did the price rise greatly. Their consumption, however, hardly affected the national diet as a whole."

In the heady days of 1946, with a socialist government in power, this tone doubtless won favour. So much for our lobster companion on the back seat. Of course in practice this meant that yet again those who could afford the best did so, and those who could not went without, or the housewife exercised her ingenuity. In a later paragraph she is duly singled out for praise, and the wicked public schoolboys duly chastised: "The war taught many housewives the art of making a little go a long way and of turning out simple dishes attractively served. Institutions were slower than housewives to alter their habits, and often failed to find substitutes for old dishes that were no longer available. One public school, for example, did not draw its full cheese ration calculated to replace a shortage of meat because it had never served cooked cheese dishes, and uncooked cheese was not particularly relished by the boys. ... New foods from America; spiced ham, commonly known as 'Spam', and dried eggs, at first looked on with suspicion, soon came to be welcomed, while other more traditional foods, such as bananas, were almost forgotten."

Noel Barber, in his London Letter in *The Overseas Daily Mail* of 22nd November, 1941, told how he almost became the proud possessor of one hundred bananas – improbably grown in Brighton by the mother of a lieutenant-commander – which were auctioned at the Stock Exchange for an "aid to Russia" fund. Mr. Barber went armed with £5, but the bananas were sold for 300 guineas. Such efforts to raise money became quite common, and included the auction, under the auspices of the Red Cross Agricultural Fund, of seats for the Victory Parade, as well as seats for the first post-war Boat Race and Wimbledon.

With conditions as they were, it is not surprising that profiteering took place, both on a small scale and on a commercial scale. Substitutes were one of the more lucrative lines, and at one stage there seemed to be a substitute for almost everything. It was forbidden to sell cream in 1940. (The author remembers a small tin of cream being produced from out of the larder. No doubt it had been jealously guarded from earlier days. The label was red with a white cow on it. It was really wasted on us. In any case, we had perfectly good fresh milk, with a good top to it.) The ministry again handed out its recrimination: "Among the first [substitutes] to appear were egg substitutes, consisting mostly of baking powder coloured yellow, and milk substitutes, consisting mostly of flour. These were followed by a large variety of so-called fruit drinks, lemon essences and tonic wines, widely advertised by misleading statements of their value in preventing vitamin deficiencies. Even reputable firms succumbed to the popular demands and began to advertise the vitamin value of their wares." Not only did they advertise the vitamin value of their wares, they could turn their gain to patriotism as well. Above the exhortation to "Make it a 'Gin and Brit' next time" the reader discovered that he might, at the modest outlay of 4s. 6d. ($22\frac{1}{2}$p) or 5s. (25p), procure a bottle of British Vermouth: "Although X is a natural, full-strength wine produced with the same ingredients and in the same way as its Continental counterparts, X costs quite a lot less. For one reason only – *it's British.*"

After food, clothing was probably the most wanted commodity under rationing. Clothes rationing was introduced in June, 1941. Prices had been rising steeply in the trade for some time. The ministry introduced a system of points, with sixty-six points allocated to each person per year. However, exceptions were made for people who needed special clothing for their occupation. Hats were exempt. Women soon became ingenious in this, as in many other areas, at making a little go a very long way. For instance, some fabric remnants were sold by weight, and in this way a woman was able to buy a two-yard remnant for only one clothing coupon and make it into a blouse, whereas to buy a new, ready-made blouse would have required four coupons. To Sir Henry Channon, who had forty suits, the war afforded a welcome respite from tailors' bills: "The big news this morning is clothes rationing. Oliver Lyttleton is only going to allow us 66 coupons per annum. A suit takes 26. Luckily I have 40 or more. Socks will be the shortage. Apart from these, if I am not bombed, I have enough clothes to last me for years. . . ." Some materials were provided later which were "off ration". The author's family had quite a large amount of brown woollen stuff apparently permeated with tar. One of the girls had a dress made of some of it, though the snapshot of her wearing it conveys an impression of extreme discomfort. The bulk of the material remained untouched, and was only finally discarded upon moving house a few years ago. The battledress which became the wartime uniform at Buckingham Palace – it is interesting to note in this context – was only finally replaced by liveries in 1967.

Advertising, though far from being the sophisticated industry it is today, adapted itself to the war. In 1941, for example, the "two vital needs to bring victory nearer" turned out to be the X milking machine and the X artificial manure distributor. Superficially, however, things were much the same at first. Then gradually, amongst the whisky and brandy, bottles of which were depicted in the midst of a group of service hats, came the announcement that two ounces of the Doctor's Ceylon Tea – at prewar price and prewar quality, too – went much further than two ounces of ordinary tea – a sure reference to the tea ration. As the Blitz grew heavier, the theme of sleep provided ample scope for the advertisers. Horlicks became a war-time nightcap, and Ovaltine was advertised with a smiling air raid warden in the background. *Ministry of Food Facts* appeared in a series, managing to strike a rare note of unreality with their advice on how to store carrots in pyramids – "It is a wise plan to rebuild your pyramid at least once during the winter" – how to dry runner beans and what to do with cauliflower leaves. "Save food! Save money! Save cargo space for munitions!"

Even soap-makers capitalized on the war imagery. "Defeat the 'Enemy Air Force' of disease with X soap . . . You cannot fight infection with 'ack-ack' [anti-aircraft fire] but X's provides a practical defence in all conditions. . . ." A patriotic firm of fish curers in Hull was at pains to state "our entire production of Finest Smoked, Frozen and Salted Fish is at present reserved for consumption in this country, but we hope to resume trading with our many Overseas customers in the not distant future." Tucked away among the classified advertisements in one newspaper was one from a firm which offered to trace ancestors: "Claim British descent!" it urged – a comforting thought in troubled times, though effectively more of a morale booster for the beleaguered British, one would have thought.

Smokers were exhorted – in the national interest – to empty their cigarette packets at the time of purchase and leave them with their tobacconist for re-use. The paper shortage was a problem which led the government to ban the production of Christmas, birthday or greeting cards after 1941, and wrapping of articles sold in shops, apart from food. Advertising posters and show cards were to be reduced in size by half their original dimensions. Cinemas, theatres, racecourses and other places of entertainment were only allowed to exhibit ten posters to advertise one programme. No more local guide books or classified directories in which entries were paid for were permitted, and it was forbidden to tie labels onto parcels or packages unless it was impossible to write the address on the wrapping paper. Advertising circulars were banned, too, except for specific categories – for example those advertising seeds, plants and fertilizers, or the sale and loan of books.

War made its existence felt in odd ways. Towards the end of 1941 no more wooden cotton reels were produced; they were to be replaced by cardboard. This, it was said, would save the country hundreds of thousands of cubic feet of wood a year. Were we such a nation of stitchers and sewers? Artificial or costume jewellery, which in peacetime would have cost perhaps three guineas, was now valued at nineteen. Felt jewellery – necklets and earrings – at around 12s. 6d. (62½p) was a more reasonable proposition and yet another example of how the nation learned to adapt, substitute and "make do." When we were unable to buy baubles for the Christmas tree, we went out into the woods and collected pine cones and the open husks of beech nuts which we daubed with melted sealing wax.

Attractive objects would often be explained away by their owners as "pre-war". This tended to be an apology for having luxuries at a time of crisis, as well as implying criticism of the quality of wartime goods. Many people who bought new things during the war, when the regulations about wrapping of purchases was first introduced, seem to have worried that other people might see what they had bought. Today we would be far more concerned about the free licence this would apparently have given to shoplifters, especially since shoppers were in those days recommended to go out armed with cases, and to wear coats with large roomy pockets. It says much for the spirit of the times. Visually the effect in the streets of London's West End, with shoppers carrying suitcases and gas-mask cases, was one of constant mobility.

By and large, shoplifting does not seem to have increased, nor did looting present any great problem when shops were bombed, although Michael Stapleton thought otherwise: "There was a great deal said in a very stiff-upper lip way about looting, but I think a lot of people would be surprised how much casual looting went on. I don't mean that people waited for their opportunity to see that they could grab something and hung about with this expectation, but I do remember that in Chapel Street Market there was a direct hit on a double-fronted grocery store. It was next door to a branch of the butcher's shop chain that I worked for. Of course we found that we could slip out into the yard where all the dustbins were kept and the brine barrel, and step over what was left of the wall into their old store room. At that time sugar was terribly scarce, and so were fats. It was perfectly easy to extract three or four pounds of butter and several pounds of sugar and scrape the dust and charcoal off them and use them, and we did so. We didn't feel any particular shame about it. When a shop was a write-off after a direct hit from a bomb, what did it matter? It might be salvaged or it might not. In any case, salvage was always a very unpredictable outcome. It could be a tenth of what was there or it could be a hundredth." Whatever reservations one might have about the morality of such an argument, even in time of war, it is a far cry from those who deliberately sought to exploit the situation and prey on those incapacitated by the bombing.

It also seemed possible that, in their greed to enjoy mannah from heaven, people would fall victim to fiendish German plots. The Nazis were supposed to have dropped devilish bombs disguised as tins of toffees, which would explode on any unsuspecting civilian who picked them up and tried to open them. The war gave rise to hundreds of bizarre scares of this kind. Had the Germans really gone in for this in a big way, they would surely have needed a subtler cover. An acute manpower crisis meant that all manufacture of consumer goods had to be closely scrutinized; tins of toffees, hardly a common feature of the English countryside, would have looked highly suspicious if seen lying around in large numbers.

Of course consumer goods were still manufactured, but all the nation's energy had to be concentrated on helping the war effort. As the Germans swept into Western Europe and France fell, Britain witnessed a rare degree of co-operation between workers and management. Many people worked incredibly long hours, although in the end the increase in productivity tended to taper off. People were full of a new sense of urgency, however, which was in itself a valuable asset.

The number of men in the forces would clearly have to be increased. More than 1,500,000 joined up during 1940. The number joining in the third quarter of that year – 460,000 – was never improved on during the whole of the war. At 1st July, more than half the British male population between the ages of twenty and twenty-five was in uniform, and more than one-fifth of the entire male population between sixteen and forty. In August, 1940, the British army had asked for 357,000 more men in the following spring, and it then became obvious that there would be a serious manpower shortage on the home front. Sir William Beveridge, later to achieve fame as the architect of the welfare state, was asked to draw up a report based on the needs of all the vital users of manpower. He presented his findings in the December of 1940. Some 1,750,000 men and 84,000 women would be needed by the armed forces and Civil Defence between September, 1940, and the end of 1941. In addition to the 357,000 men asked for by the army for March 1941, they had asked for 100,000 each month thereafter. This could only be done if some 500,000 men were taken away from the munitions factories. But in order to provide equipment and arms for the increased forces, the munition work force had itself to be increased by almost 1,500,000. The arithmetic was impossible – resembling an ever decreasing series of concentric circles; simply by putting the basic figures down on a piece of paper it was evident that there was a wild imbalance between estimated supply and demand.

The conclusion was that more women would have to be employed. The government then set about providing the machinery for the control and distribution of manpower. No amount of control, however, could determine labour relations. In 1939 1,354,000 working days had been lost through strikes. In 1940, the year of Dunkirk, this figure was reduced to 941,000, but in 1941 it was back up to 1,077,000 and in 1942 it was more than the figure for 1939. Whatever the immediate causes of the strikes there was a plain fear in the minds of working-class people as to what would happen after the war as a result of controls. Memories of the strikes and hunger marches of the twenties and thirties were still fresh in people's minds.

Control was not only unpopular, it was incompetently carried out. It had seemed bad enough to an outsider that the government should start tinkering with the distribution of manpower at the beginning of the war, even to a fairly well-informed and public spirited Rose Macaulay: "Half the London shops are closing or closed, and their staffs sacked. And all this government-paid A.R.P. work *etc.* is taking men out of industry, and ruining the industries, and paying men out of public money. The world seems to have gone quite crazy. . . ". The A.R.P. men justified themselves several times over when the hour came, but Cecil King put his finger on much more serious faults. In July of the following year, when the nation's life seemed to hang in the balance, he learned about an industrial spy who, when war began, was asked by the Admiralty to work for them in a similar capacity in the dockyard at Devonport. In the spy's opinion there was squandering of resources and maladministration of a kind that would have been inconceivable in private industry. For example, 18,000 men were doing the work of 3,000; and a wood store was sited next to a stock of 8,000 gallons of turpentine. Despite his repeated recommendations, nothing at all was done about it. When stores were allocated for a particular job they were booked out and, if they were not required on that job after all, they were simply thrown away or stolen. After seven months of mounting frustration he resigned.

The newspapers were in a difficult situation. If similar examples were brought to light and investigated, they were on the horns of a moral dilemma as to whether or not to make their findings public. The government was acutely sensitive to "unpatriotic" criticism. Already *The Daily Mirror* had incurred official displeasure through several of its stories and campaigns – not least the one against the "Colonel Blimps" in the army, and the persistence of what the *Mirror* regarded as outdated attitudes and routines. Quite often, however, the *Mirror* was right, both in the army and in the factory. One of its reporters, investigating reports of lack of organization, entered the Vickers-Armstrong works at Barrow unchallenged. He simply put on overalls and a cap and spent the whole day wandering around the plant. He went aboard a new aircraft carrier, again unchallenged, and reckoned that seventy-five per cent of the men he saw there were doing nothing. Yet the factory was working two ten-and-a-half-hour shifts seven days a week at the time. Undoubtedly there was maladministration, and waste of money and manpower on a large scale. Fewer and shorter shifts could probably have been worked without much fall in output. Money was certainly made on contracts which ought never to have been signed, even in peacetime with normal competition, let alone in war and when the country was in so much danger. Nevertheless, hundreds and thousands made an immense personal effort and sacrifice. It would also seem to imply that every single member of the population should have been prepared to forget the social injustices, the hardship, the bitterness of the previous decades, virtually overnight. For a moment, for that finest hour, perhaps, people were. Only too soon did the hour pass, however, and human nature reassert itself.

The consumer society has advanced a long way since then. Indeed it is still tightening its hold on Western society. Its values are totally opposed to those of older generations and those who were brought up during the last war. No longer do we buy shoes to be repaired and worn for a number of years. Rather than repair them once or twice it is cheaper to buy a new pair of shoes. Even more contrary is the whole commercial philosophy of stimulated demand. The lack of variety or choice during the war has meant that older people are sometimes bewildered by the array of consumer goods available today – especially when many of them are beyond their means. It is refreshing that some younger people have seriously questioned these consumer values, to the point of rejecting them, though how effective their protest will be in the long run remains to be seen.

One cannot put back the clock, but did we really struggle from World War Two only to clothe ourselves with a shell of ever bigger and better motor cars, or to smother ourselves with the indestructible foam of ever more powerful detergents?

4. Relaxation and Communication

"I would say to the House, as I said to those
who have joined this Government, 'I have nothing
to offer but blood, toil, tears and sweat'."

Winston Churchill 13 May 1940

"Roll out the Barrel, we'll have a barrel of fun.
Roll out the Barrel, we've got the blues on the run . . .".

Words of a popular song

Immediately after Neville Chamberlain had issued Britain's declaration of war in 1939, government radio announcements stated that all cinemas, theatres and other places of entertainment were to be closed down at once; race meetings, football matches and similar mass meetings were forbidden. This was in line with the official policy of dispersal, but when no bombs fell and no military news appeared, it became clear, even to government officials, that needless tension might quickly destroy national morale. Closely related to the question of morale was that of commercial interest. Indeed, for some people the two were synonymous.

All artistic activity virtually came to a halt overnight. Theatre and opera artistes, dance bandsmen and orchestral performers found themselves facing instant dismissal. Gloom fell upon the world of entertainment and sport. Famous companies and orchestras were to be disbanded, whole football teams joined the army. The manager of one of London's biggest West End ballrooms told the social research unit Mass Observation: "We closed on 3rd September. In the morning we listened to the broadcast, and I called in what members of the staff there were to hear it. After the speech we realized we couldn't keep on. I told them the situation, and we all went into the ballroom and started taking the glass tops off the tables and clearing the room, making it ready as an air-raid shelter."

But when the government began to relax the regulations, business began to boom. In fact by November, 1939, some dance halls were doing better business than they had before the outbreak of war. The blackout helped, since people could no longer simply go out for the evening and stroll around from place to place. They needed somewhere to go, and once they arrived they usually stayed for the evening. Of course transport problems tended to keep people at home, especially when petrol was rationed. But even this did not deter an elderly couple who used to visit a south London dance hall regularly from their home in Croydon, three nights a week. Much to the manager's surprise, they arrived next time on bicycles. The Locarno, Streatham Hill, advertised "dancing as usual during alterations in Europe," and the Jitterbug Marathon at the Paramount, Tottenham Court Road, on 20th November attracted a crowd of 1,400 or more. A new dance was devised, named the Blackout Stroll; "Knees up, Mother Brown," which the b.b.c. had previously hinted that they would be unable to broadcast if a certain music publisher produced it, became an all-time hit.

As to the songs which people sang in the first two years of war, these were very different from those of 1914. There were hardly any patriotic songs as such, and none of the "jingoism" of the Great War. "There'll always be an England" was an early exception – it was a best-seller by mid-November, 1939 – but far more typical of the atmosphere of this war was "We're gonna hang out the washing on the Siegfried Line". *The Daily Telegraph* warned the nation, on 6th October: "The incorrigible flippancy of the new British war song . . . has given great offence to Germany. Indignant references have been made to it in the German propaganda wireless broadcast in English. The statement by the b.b.c. that the song was written by men of anti-aircraft units is said, by the German wireless, to be obviously untrue. 'This is not a soldiers' song, because soldiers do not brag,' it was stated. 'It was not written in the soldiers' camps, but by the Jewish scribes of the b.b.c. The Englishman's washing will be very dirty before they come anywhere near the Siegfried Line.' " The apparent refusal of the Germans to believe that it was a soldiers' song – apart from the fact that it did not coincide with their own very clear idea of what a soldiers' song should be – lay in the fact that no British soldiers had been seen near the Siegfried Line. They had, on the other hand, been seen in Paris, where their arrival – according to German radio – was greeted as a return to "the good old days when rich young Americans spent money like water." Lord Haw Haw soon produced his version of the song for his broadcasts to England.

Interestingly, a second type of war song – with absence, remembrance and return as the theme – appeared early on, and in particular "We'll meet again". This probably deserves the title of signature tune of World War Two, as sung by Vera Lynn, if any one tune does. "Lilli Marlene" probably overcame national barriers to a much greater degree, but even so it was not an English song, and never lost its German associations.

Towards the end of 1941, however, a new tendency was apparent, and the most popular records in November show that the public's taste had changed.

Their Finest Hour

People wanted something different, something slightly exotic, to take them out of themselves for a while. "Coral Sea" and "Under a Blanket of Blue", played by the Casa Loma Orchestra, represented a far cry from the reality of wartime winter. There was an upsurge of Hawaiian music at this time, too. It was novel, and caught on fast, and was certainly exotic. Roland Peachy brought out "South Sea Lullabies" and "Serenade of the Islands"; Johnny Pineapple made "Kakohi" and "Fair Hawaii", and a gentleman called Felix Mendelssohn produced "Aloha Oe" and "Song of the Islands".

The theatres and opera houses found themselves in a similar situation to the dance halls. Sadlers Wells closed immediately, but an experimental matinee performance of *Faust* was staged on the afternoon of Saturday 30th September, 1939, and was a great success. The experiment was repeated first once a week, and later twice a week. By January, 1940, the Carl Rosa Company had reopened and began to make very successful provincial tours. By the summer of 1940 Sadlers Wells Ballet (eventually to become the Royal Ballet), and its opera company, together with various other companies in and around London, were playing to full houses every night of the week.

In the eventful first week of September, 1940, the D'Oyly Carte Opera Company, who had been playing in Hammersmith and Streatham, were at Golders Green before embarking on a tour of the provinces. In the West End a new Mickey Rooney film, with Virginia Weidler, *Young Tom Edison*, had just opened, and on Saturday night – that memorable night of 7th September – Sadlers Wells were performing *Faust* once more at their home in Roseberry Avenue, ironically perhaps. As the audience spilled out into the North London street after the performance and looked East, the sky was ablaze with the fires in the City of London and the docks. Another dramatic halt was put to performances. But this time the theatre was turned into a rest centre for evacuees, and the Company disbanded. The Carl Rosa Company, then playing at the People's Palace, Whitechapel, lost all its scenery and costumes a few days later, situated as it was in the East End. Covent Garden Opera House was turned into a dance hall.

The formation of the Council for the Encouragement of Music and the Arts – from which the present Arts Council is directly descended – helped Sadlers Wells to keep going after its disbandment by keeping a nucleus of personnel and taking opera on tour. The entire Sadlers Wells Company then numbered twenty-five, including the orchestra. The conductor filled out the band parts at the piano, and chorus members helped with the scenery, lighting and costumes. The venture was so successful that the Company was enlarged; more provincial tours were made, to places where opera had never been seen or heard of before, and a headquarters was set up for Sadler Wells at the New Theatre in London. The Carl Rosa Company struggled back onto its feet, too, eventually, and the present excellence of British ballet and opera may well be traced back to those rugged days. Opera in particular, which had always been a somewhat foreign element in British cultural life, at last began to take root in native soil.

One theatre alone did not close, indeed it made the fact its motto. The Windmill Theatre – "We Never Closed" – kept its doors open throughout the war. However what Hitler's bombs were unable to do, changing public taste finally achieved. The Windmill's particular brand of entertainment – scantily clad girls and revue-style comedians – was slowly and inexorably abandoned, left like some extinct animal in a glass case. Several famous comics made their names at the Windmill, and it was a wonderful school for them. When an air raid warning went during one performance the entire audience filed out, save for one man who, it transpired, was deaf.

On the sports front the tale was less bright. Racing was very badly hit, and even by the end of 1941 it was only permitted on Saturdays. The National Hunt Meeting at Cheltenham, which would normally have lasted two days, was thus spread out over two weeks. The government limited the number of jumpers to be trained across the entire country to 700 for the season, though it seems as if there were at least 900 in training, according to informed sources. An item "from a military camp in the north", which almost got lost in the news towards the end of 1941, concerned a "prolific young run-getter, Len Hutton, who made a record knock of 364 against Australia at the Oval in 1938." Many sportsmen joined the services immediately, which, apart from the effects of government regulations and restrictions on travel disrupted clubs and leagues seriously.

As Mass Observation pointed out in their analysis of the situation in sport, the government would have done far better to donate the £50,000 they spent on a poster campaign – urging the nation to be cheerful – to sport. For as Mass Observation well realized, sport – and football in particular – gave some excitement to the dull lives of the working classes. Only the onset of the Blitz seems to have been anything like so powerful a contender as a distraction for those left at home. The effect of the war on sport need not have been so marked so soon. For one thing, the manpower crisis was not to make itself felt for at least a year. But influenced by patriotic fervour, some clubs encouraged their players to join up, and the whole of the Arsenal and Queen's Park Rangers soccer teams went in one fell swoop. Many spectators, too, had to work overtime in munitions factories, or had Home Guard or A.R.P. duties which drastically curtailed their free time. Others simply could not afford to attend matches as the manpower switch from non-strategic employment began to operate and they found themselves for the moment unemployed.

Another temporary, but highly effective, reason for falling attendances was the fact that the evacuation of wives with children meant that men had to cook their own meals and do the shopping and household chores. Also, the weekend was the only time many men were able to visit their distant families. The break up of families in this way, and the absence of sons and husbands in the forces, created a general lack of incentive to go out, especially in view of the fact that one might well arrive at a football ground to find that the match was off, or the crowd limit imposed by the government had been reached, and the gates shut. Another difficulty was that teams were not allowed to travel more than fifty miles for away-games. Sometimes, however, the dislocation of war time traffic overruled everything. The Nottingham Forest team set off to play Norwich but somehow ended up at Louth instead. In the New Year a Press campaign urged the government to relax restrictions; but the fundamental problem of the danger of large concentrations of people in the open air was one which would remain until the end of the war. By slightly easing restrictions and organizing more localized league football, some improvement was effected.

What, one wonders, would have been the effect on the nation's morale if television had been as advanced in 1939 as it is today? On 1st September, 1939, the B.B.C.'s television service at Alexandra Palace in London closed down. Its transmissions might have guided enemy aircraft. Had viewing been at today's peak, and television still been obliged to go off the air, one wonders how the nation would have reacted. As it was, the loss of the television broadcasts in 1939 was no great hardship. The radio, however, was a very different matter. The same problem existed, namely that German pilots might be able to use B.B.C. transmitters to pinpoint their targets more accurately. A solution was devised involving the use of a number of low-powered transmitters throughout the country, and a number of lorries carrying transmitters to complete the network. When an air raid warning went out, the B.B.C. standard transmitters either shut down completely or reduced their power considerably. This meant that reception at ground level was scarcely altered, but that transmission would not be picked up in the air and so used as a navigational aid by the enemy.

Only a skeleton staff was left in London at B.B.C. headquarters. The main broadcasting was carried on from Bristol, Manchester and Wood Norton, near Evesham. In the days of the phoney war, when all places of entertainment were closed, the B.B.C. played a magnificent role, and continued to do so throughout the war. Its news bulletins were eagerly listened in to by people not only in Britain itself, but wherever they could be picked up overseas, and where often it was a serious crime to do so. The B.B.C. built up an enviable reputation for the standard of its reporting – even when it was obliged to censor itself severely. The lack of definite news on the B.B.C. may account for the success of Lord Haw Haw, whose propaganda broadcasts from Nazi Germany were designed to mislead the British and undermine their morale. It has been estimated that a third of all radio listeners in Britain heard him. There was a terrible fascination in this, mixed strongly with repulsion; Haw Haw seemed to tell people things that the British government failed to tell them. During 1940 the number of people listening to him tailed away. By then things had begun to happen, and the war was no longer phoney. Besides which, the B.B.C. had found the answer to Lord Haw Haw. Official attempts at propaganda had not been very successful. It is not a thing which comes very easily to the British, and was consequently even less successful when directed at their own people. Perhaps without realizing it the B.B.C. had hit on a most spectacular piece of propaganda: ITMA.

In July, 1939, there had been a band show called *It's That Man Again*, with the comedian Tommy Handley as compère. It was not very successful. At the outbreak of war the producer, Francis Worsley, had a brilliant idea. ITMA became re-incarnate as a zany send-up of war – on both sides of the Channel. The Germans could never have countenanced this, but it brought a breath of sanity into the unreality of the phoney war, and support in the dark days beyond. As Worsley wrote: "At a time when everybody in the land, from the highest administrator down to the humblest A.R.P. type, was being given a new title which generally resolved itself into the appropriate initials, we thought it would be in keeping if we made Tommy a V.I.P. of some sort. We decided that nothing less than Cabinet rank would meet the case, so we created the post of Minister of Aggravation and Mysteries, housed in the Office of Twerps."

As an example of the sort of exchange, here is a telephone conversation between the Minister (Tommy Handley) and Funf (Jack Train talking into a tumbler), "the enemy agent with feet of sauerkraut," who was a combination of Lord Haw Haw and Hitler:

"Who's speaking?"

"Funf."

"Funf? Is that a name or a rude expression?"

"It is Funf, your favourite spy."

"It may be Funf for you, but it's not much funf for me . . ."

"I have found out everything."

"Everything? Well, where can I get enough petrol for my cigarette lighter?"

"Do not leave your office – your life is in danger."

"Nonsense, I'm wearing my steel singlet and my shell-proof shorts. They'll never puncture my prerogative." It sounds rather corny now, but when delivered by Tommy Handley with expert timing, the effect was very funny.

Winston Churchill's stirring speeches were first heard by most people via the radio, though with varying results as we have seen elsewhere. Almost as popular a broadcaster was the plain-speaking Yorkshire novelist J. B. Priestley, who seemed to epitomise the attitudes of many British people. The sort of things he said were usually the things they would have said, and how they would have liked to have said them, had they been given the chance and, incidentally, had the ability. Priestley was not all things to all men, by any means, and some of his comments on the inequality and privilege he saw around him cannot have pleased everyone. But it was good that such feelings were aired. Another programme to enjoy considerable popularity, surprisingly perhaps, was a discussion programme called *The Brains Trust*. But for the nation at large, the B.B.C.'s output of music was probably most appreciated, especially *Music while you work*, for example, when relayed to the factory floor.

The whole of the B.B.C. music department was moved out of London with the first wholesale evacuation of personnel, but in late 1941 all the music department, together with religious broadcasting, was brought together. For security reasons the location was not announced to the public, so the news item was simply headed – somewhat coyly – from "a south of England town": "Wherever you walk you see musicians. You bump into bassoons, jolt against 'cellos. The B.B.C. have settled musicians, technicians and administrative staff here. For studios they have taken over the corn exchange, a billiards hall, a school hall, a church hall and a chapel. Among the musicians are the ninety-two members of the B.B.C. Symphony Orchestra, and one of the aims of the move is to keep up and if possible improve the supply of good music."

One must not imagine, however, that the whole nation was glued to the radio and devoured the newspapers whenever they could. It was estimated that as late as 1943 half the troops stationed in Great Britain alone did not see a daily newspaper or listen regularly to the news on the radio. And of course what news there was – and there was precious little during the phoney war – was censored. The question of censorship is always a difficult one, but during World War Two the British Government seems to have been particularly inept. Shortly after the outbreak of war an American correspondent in London asked one of the censors at the Ministry of Information (before Duff Cooper took over) for the text of a propaganda leaflet which had been dropped over Germany. He was told that the Ministry was unable to disclose information which might be of value to the enemy. The correspondent then pointed out that two million of the leaflets had been dropped on Germany. On another occasion *The Daily Mirror*, having covered a visit by King George VI to a tank factory, submitted its photographs to the censor, who passed them. It was then noticed by the newspaper that the photograph showed quite clearly new improvements to the model of tank being made in that particular factory, and therefore of vital importance to national security. In this case the newspaper censored itself.

It was the arbitrary or haphazard nature of censorship which irritated people. Typical of a news handout in 1941 was the following: "Flashes from anti-aircraft guns lit up the Thames Estuary on two nights during this week. Bombs were dropped by enemy raiders on one occasion, but no damage was done. The raiders were turned back before they reached the capital, where once again no alarm was heard. Raids over Britain generally were on a small scale. Single raiders dropped bombs in south-east England. Some houses were damaged and there were a few casualties. Two enemy bombers were destroyed off the east coast of England. A D.F.C. squadron-leader pilot accounted for one of them. He was carrying out a practice flight a few miles off the north-east coast when he sighted a JU 88 flying very fast. He attacked it and sent it crashing into the sea." Somewhere, someone may have thought that this was what people wanted – or expected – to read. The air of nonchalance sounds too good to be true. This sort of thing must have inevitably forced readers to query the selectivity of the news given them. It was especially worrying for people living away from home, or for those who had a family living in a particular area where only the vaguest news was given about raids. In such circumstances it might have been better to omit such references altogether. At least people would then have known that it was being deliberately suppressed.

The selective news was bad enough, but doctored news was even worse. Apparently the Germans were in the habit of shooting down the barrage balloons over Dover almost daily in the weeks before the Blitz. In a story for the newspaper submitted by a *Mirror* correspondent, he mentioned forty balloons, which the censor amended to two. Everyone in Dover knew the real number, so that readers of *The Mirror* there would be baffled by the report. Of course the proportion of the total number of *Mirror* readers in and around Dover must have been a mere fraction of a per cent. Even so, if this sort of thing happened often and throughout the country, something on the lines of a national crisis of confidence might have developed.

Luckily for *The Daily Mirror* its readers, and indeed most newspaper readers, have a touching faith in the printed word, a faith which some journalists might well consider before they give vent to their prose. But there were those who saw the funnier side of the business, and took it all in good part. On a day late in 1941 when the prospect of invasion seemed remote, Britain's only weather news allowed by security was that mild weather had prevailed in the Strait of Dover on that day. Which provoked one poetic commentator to observe:

> "We can't inform the Germans what
> Climatic states in Britain reign,
> But if invasion still may come
> You'd think it would be fairly plain

Their Finest Hour

That it is tempting evil Fate
To say it's calmer in the Strait."

If anything, the government was far too sensitive in this field. They were particularly sensitive to the possible existence of a Fifth Column, and various campaigns were carried out to check careless talk. Indeed, it was made a punishable offence to cause alarm or despondency, with a fine of up to fifty pounds. Overseas mail and telephone trunk lines were censored and tapped respectively from September, 1939, which was a sensible precaution, though even then, a little late in the day. Such precautions and penalties seemed hard to bear in the days of phoney war, and were correspondingly attenuated. There definitely were instances of subversive activities, and information may well have been gleaned by spies through careless talk. But considering how open the situation was in many other respects, in the end there seemed little point in oppressing the public at large.

Ultimately it was not so much what might or might not be given away by uncensored accounts – Cecil King was particularly sad that an embargo on spy news stories prevented the *Mirror* from printing a marvellous story about a spy who passed secret information cut up in small pieces and inserted in batches of meat pies – but the fact that Churchill was so sensitive to what he chose to call the national interest, but what really amounted to criticism of his administration. Churchill was particularly angry when one of his own books was quoted against him by Hugh Cudlipp, the editor of the *Mirror*. Rather than handle the whole business himself, and so give the impression of a personal vendetta, Churchill delegated the matter to Clement Attlee. In the event the whole thing went off at less than half-cock, since Attlee – given the job of rebuking those responsible – found it a chore which he neither relished nor was suited to. There is hardly any wonder, since it was patently a case of Churchill's wounded pride.

It is interesting that as early as 1941 Churchill's speeches were being marketed on gramophone record, as was Lynn Fontanne "the magnificent American actress . . . who speaks the charming words beautifully." The charming words were those of a rather bad extended poem by Alice Miller entitled *The White Cliffs*. It was first published in England on 13th February, 1941, and was in its eighth edition by July of that year, having run through two editions that April and May. It reached the 19th (illustrated) edition by 1943.

The poem tells the story of an American woman who marries an Englishman, bears him a son, and is then widowed in the war. The verse is indifferent, but it put into words what many Americans felt (in America it went into eleven editions between 16th September and 12th December, 1940), and what many English people wanted Americans to feel. Its propaganda value was surely considerable. The closing lines give an indication of the tone and message of the poem:

"I am an American bred,
  I have seen much to hate here – much to forgive,
  But in a world where England is finished and dead,
  I do not wish to live."

Luckily the last war did not produce the sort of poetry that came out of World War One. A writer considering this in 1940 reckoned that it was because, until then, so few people had been killed. His cynicism was happily not confirmed; the later years of the war did not bring a crop of moist-eyed verse as in World War One. Surely one of the saddest examples must have been Rupert Brooke's sonnet *Peace*, from 1914:

"Now, God be thanked Who has matched us with His hour,
  And caught our youth, and wakened us from sleeping,
  With hand made sure, clear eye, and sharpened power,
  To turn, as swimmers, into cleanness leaping,
  Glad from a world grown old and cold and weary,
  Leave the sick hearts that honour could not move,
  And half-men, and their dirty songs and dreary,
  And all the little emptiness of love! . . ."

Can anyone ever have gone into war – that war in particular – or even contemplated doing so, for such patently misguided motives? Quite apart from the quality of the verse, one should be relieved that the complexion of World War Two literature was not like that.

It would nevertheless be difficult to point to an example of the "best" literature of the last war. The war simply did not take people in the way the previous one did. In any case Wilfred Owen had already revealed in his verse what the realities of the first war were. One could do worse than take virtually any number of *The Penguin New Writing*, edited by John Lehmann. Some of the contributors have since become the gods of literature. Others have sunk without trace, but the overall impression is that of an optic which was not distorted by "poetic" sentiment or patriotism. As an example of verse there are several poems of Stephen Spender which convey the spirit, or indeed of Edith Sitwell. One in particular is reasonably significant, since it has subsequently been set to music by Benjamin Britten, whose *War Requiem* – inspired by both wars – has become a classic in its own time, and may turn out to be one of the great works of art inspired by twentieth-century war. One fears that its early popularity may warrant a reappraisal fairly soon, since immediate acclaim in art – but particularly in music – can be a two-edged sword. The *War Requiem* may possibly appear to future generations as the coda to World War Two. If so, then *Still Falls the Rain* must surely be the heart of the opus. It is subtitled "The Raids 1940. Night and Dawn.":

Their Finest Hour

> "Still falls the Rain –
> Dark as the world of man, black as our loss –
> Blind as the nineteen hundred and forty nails
> Upon the Cross . . .
> On Dives and on Lazarus:
> Under the Rain the sore and the gold are as one . . .
> Still falls the Rain –
> Then – O Ile leape up to my God: who pulls me doune –
> See, see where Christ's blood streames in the firmament:
> It flows from the Brow we nailed upon the tree
> Deep to the dying, to the thirsting heart
> That holds the fires of the world – dark, smirched with pain
> As Caesar's laurel crown . . ."

For more literature directly inspired by the war, or deeply influenced by it, Elizabeth Bowen's novel *The Heat of the Day*, which is quoted elsewhere in this book, is well worth reading. It deals not with the war as an end in itself, but with human relationships set against the background of the war. The war is therefore seen by the author and characters – and so ultimately the reader – in a fresh contemporary light. Here is just such an experience, that of a man in the street during a raid: "Harrison, back again, stood in the middle of a street, otherwise empty, illuminated by a chandelier flare. During the pulse of silence between the overhead throbbing and the bark of the guns, the flare made the street like a mirrored drawing-room. Above where Harrison stood peering at something jotted on an envelope, white-green incandescence flowed from the lovely shapely symbol, which slowly descended as it died – the sky to the east reflected flamingo-pink nobody could have taken to be the dawn; the west was jagged with flames. Ostensibly the population of London was underground: now and then could be heard an important clanging of NFS or ambulance bells; once or twice a private car shot past. Bombardment reopened upon Harrison doggedly footing it in the direction of Stella's new flat, automatically swerving clear of buildings liable at any time to be struck and fall."

This is, of course, a work of fiction. In real life not everyone had such experiences, nor saw them in the same way, nor was so articulate about them. But if Churchill's impression of "their finest hour" is to be taken at face value, then *The Heat of the Day* may be as well. In addition to literature directly related to the war there was a wide variety of books published in its early months. *How Green was My Valley* by Richard Llewellyn, *Good-bye to Berlin* by Christopher Isherwood, *Finnegan's Wake*, by James Joyce, and *The Grapes of Wrath* by John Steinbeck – these make an interesting quartet available to the reader during the phoney war.

There were some fascinating films, too. *The Lady Vanishes* starring Michael Redgrave and Margaret Lockwood, *Ninotchka* starring Greta Garbo, *Wuthering Heights* starring Laurence Olivier, David Niven and Merle Oberon, *Nurse Cavell* starring Anna Neagle, *Pinocchio*, and *Pygmalion* starring Wendy Hiller and Leslie Howard, are a few of the successes of the early months of the war. Leslie Howard played in several propaganda films and died in 1943 when his plane was shot down. Leslie Henson went on packing them into the theatres until the Blitz temporarily put a stop to a lot of entertainment. There were many more wartime favourites who carried on. Others stayed in America, claiming that they were of more use there, and this was no doubt true to a large extent. With literary figures such as W. H. Auden, Christopher Isherwood and Aldous Huxley the problem was different. Harold Nicolson was asked to write an article condemning them, but he refused to do so – not only because he was personally involved, but because he admired their intellects. The climate of 1914 no longer prevailed. Very few white feathers were handed out this time.

The poetic documentary films of Humphrey Jennings, in particular *London Can Take it* (1940), *Listen to Britain* (1942) and, from the closing months of the war, *Diary for Timothy* (1945), are fascinating essays. They are relatively free from patriotic sentiment. Indeed the fact that E. M. Forster wrote the script of *Diary for Timothy* gives an indication of the line it takes. These films may be criticized for not showing the grim realities of war, but one must remember that many different kinds of reality existed during the war. A handling of the grim realities of war could be as unrealistic as an Ivor Novello musical: "When I visited the city a day or two later . . . an incident, to me charming, occurred. It was the dinner-hour, and a very pretty young girl ran up to the car and threw a box of cigars into it. . . . The gift must have cost her two or three pounds. I was very glad (in my official capacity) to give her a kiss. I then went on to see the long mass grave in which so many citizens and their children had been newly buried. The spirit of Birmingham shone brightly, and its million inhabitants, highly organized, conscious and comprehending, rode high above their physical suffering." The author was that well-known realist, Winston Churchill.

The strength of the Jennings documentaries – technical and artistic merits apart – lies in the wide area of wartime life that he covers. He does not shirk such issues as the fear of unemployment which followed World War One, and was a very real threat to workers in the next war. He frequently makes brilliantly telling points simply by cutting in to one shot from another, and juxtaposing his material to great effect. His films are also essentially human in their approach, which makes one feel that they are all very real. They convey the immediate quality that life had then, whether it be an elderly arthritic couple crouching under a table as the bombs drop, or whether it be the atmosphere at one of Myra Hess's lunchtime concerts in the denuded National Gallery in London.

To some it seemed paradoxical that a bomb might drop as they sat and listened to Beethoven – or indeed that Beethoven should be performed at all. It never even occurred to others. The essential thing was that, in the horror and discomfort, a window should be kept open to show what Western civilization had achieved, not what she was in the process of destroying. Whether it was Beethoven – or any other composer – in the National Gallery, or a piano or gramophone in the underground, music was a vital element of hope.

Some of the London underground stations became regular hives of entertainment and recreation. Church services were held there and one even produced its own magazine, *The Swiss Cottager*. Library facilities and film shows were laid on, and concert parties and drama companies performed.

In the early months of the war culture had tended to take a hard knock. So much is made clear in *War Begins at Home*, the Mass Observation report edited by Tom Harrisson and Charles Madge. As a contemporary document it makes illuminating reading, but since it was published in 1940 it only shows the conditions prior to bombing. Apart from government closure of places of entertainment, libraries were commandeered for the administration of such things as ration books, and museums and galleries were emptied of their treasures. As early as 1933 several institutions responsible for safeguarding valuable objects had been looking for suitable hiding places. Some of these caches have never been revealed – presumably some of them could be used again if need arose. The British Museum did not begin its evacuation until 24th August, 1939. The operation was carried out quite speedily, however, so that if invasion had come, it could presumably have been brought forward easily enough.

But if art and literature – that great river of human communication – suffered severely, a smaller channel – the post – did not. Telephone lines tended to suffer, but one of the most amazing things about the war was the fact that the postal service worked, and continued to work, remarkably well. Newspapers and magazines kept afloat, too, and this in itself was no mean feat. But when one thinks that it was possible at the height of the Blitz to send fresh fruit and vegetables from one end of England to the other, right into the heart of London, and without damage or delay, then the Post Office was really worthy of praise. The prime minister despatched a memo to the postmaster-general on 19th September, 1940: "There are considerable complaints about the Post Office service during air raids. Perhaps you will give me a report on what you are doing." This was at the height of the Blitz, and it was less than two weeks' old. Four days later Rose Macaulay could write to her sister: "Thank you so much for your card – almost a miracle, for it left

Romford early this morning and reached me this afternoon." Either the prime minister was simply retailing someone else's unlucky experience, or the postmaster-general acted amazingly quickly.

Could the appendix to Churchill's *History of the Second World War*, which contains the minutes and telegrams, have been deliberately included to redress the balance when the main text gets too remote – especially since many of the items are quite unrelated to anything in the main text? They paint a picture of a prime minister concerned with the smallest details of daily life – an impression which is generally sadly lacking from the main text and which, if it was genuine in intent, often failed to materialize in practice.

Those lofty commands which actually contained such phrases as, "Pray let me have, on one sheet of paper . . ." – or, "Let a report be prepared on two sheets only . . ." – make astonishing reading. Shivers must have run down the spines of the recipients. There is a defiant flamboyancy in the inclusion of this one to General Ismay on 11th December, 1940: "Let models be made of Rhodes and Leros. Report when they will be ready." If only one of the memos had said "Let the people be properly cared for."

5. Some Social Effects of the War

"After the last war statesmen promised 'Homes
Fit for Heroes to Live In' because the phrase was
a vote-catcher and because men in uniform
were to be bought by gratuities and promises. This
time it is not just the men in khaki to whom
they have to answer, but to every man, woman,
and child . . .".   Ritchie Calder *The Lesson of London*

Whenever World War Two is mentioned amongst a group of people who lived through it, seldom can any of them resist telling some of his or her favourite personal stories. Such conversations are a sure sign that, for many people, the war was the most exciting time of their life, and stands out in technicolour against the monochrome of much that went before and came after.

Such a profound experience must have had far-reaching effects on the lives of people there and then, and consequences for the life of the nation at large. How permanent they were is another matter, but people adapted quickly and with a minimum of fuss. A lady who otherwise would probably not have taken to wearing trousers, took to the idea very easily when she found that she had to work at a rest centre on twenty-four-hour shifts, and sleep in the same room as the male members of her shift: "I am just off to buy some slacks. They seem the most sensible garment for a communal sleeping apartment."

The rest centres in London were a distillation of what happened to life in the Blitz: "About a fortnight ago during a very lively raid we heard and felt a mighty crash. Two or three houses nearby had been hit and presently about twenty people were brought to the centre very shaken and very dirty. Later on the wardens came in to tell a young man that his father and mother and two other relations had all been killed. As soon as billets can be found or homes repaired the people leave the centre. The wet weather is finding out the weak places in the roofs and ceilings so more people are coming in because their homes are so damp. Among others we have had dogs, cats, a parakeet and tame mice."

One imagines waves of human flotsam and jetsam washed up in the wake of every raid: experiences from death to tame mice crammed in the space of a few lines. But people took it all in their stride. The mother of the writer of the two letters quoted above – no longer young then – adapted quickly to life in the Blitz: "We got to church yesterday, and had a warning midday, just at the Consecration – but hardly any one left – same at Evensong. . . . All Clear, so I am off to shops . . .". The nuns apparently, too: "It is most amusing here, the Sisters at St. George's have given up their sitting room to the Royal Army Medical Corps men at the House of Mercy and entertain them with music and refreshments, and have a sleeping room in the basement for air wardens, *etc*. They are getting quite gay . . .".

The change from routine, the unexpected complexion of life, evoked a remarkable response from people. Even a wedding – usually the object of weeks and even months of planning – had to be improvised in wartime: "The father, mother and bride motored up from Hampshire and had lunch here, but no bridegroom or brother arrived. We all waited in St. James's from 4.30 to 5.30 then went into the vicarage for tea. Still no bridegroom. At 5.40 he arrived, half dead and distracted, and we returned to church and had a very nice service and they were man and wife before six – and the service continued. At the last the brother, an officer in the Hants Regiment, arrived and they all five started in the motor for Winchester and did not get into any hotel till nearly midnight. . . . The menfolk only had twenty-four hours' leave. The bride started work in the bank on Monday morning and the bridegroom went off to his ship at Portsmouth."

These were but short-term effects of the war. Few of them can have had any lasting effect on daily life, unless it was the ability to adapt more readily to circumstances. To take one example, the enormous increase since then in the number of labour-saving devices in the average home, and the developments in the production and distribution of foodstuffs, must have swamped any such ability long ago. One very appreciable effect in the short term which may well have had a radical long-term effect, was a breakdown of many of the sexual and moral barriers. In the words of the official pamphlet: "Social conditions in England and Wales during the years 1939 to 1945 have favoured the spread of venereal disease far more than in the years 1914–18. Apart from the fact that country areas have been invaded by huge numbers of war workers and evacuees, families have been disrupted to a much greater degree than previously, and owing to the fact that the country has been a training ground and a base for the forces of other nations, besides our own, sexual promiscuity must have been practised on a scale never previously attained in this country."

This is the clinical aspect, put in a rather clinical way. It manifested itself in much more visible and human terms, however. In *War over West Ham* Doreen Idle revealed how far there had been a breakdown – in West Ham at least – of traditional *mores*: "Neighbours of either sex frequently throw in their lot together. A woman will live with her neighbour who is a small shopkeeper, looking after his domestic affairs; a man and a woman who work together during the day will also share their home arrangements and their shelter; those who are the sole remaining members of evacuated families pool their domestic resources."

If this seems to smack somewhat of the siege of Leningrad by English standards, it must be borne in mind that West Ham was a rather extreme situation. Even so, the Blitz broke down quite a lot of reserve. Not long before it began, Cecil King was motoring west out of London when he saw a woman waiting for a lift. In spite of six air raid alarms, the planes up in the sky and the guns firing off all around, she refused to accept a lift from him, a strange man. As King pointed out, it would need a "very persistent philanderer indeed to attempt anything in an 8 h.p. Ford under the circumstances." Things certainly did change, but how radically is another matter. Nowadays, in the "permissive society", one is tempted to discern the logical culmination of the revolution which began during the war. In the long term this *may* be true, but if so, then there *was* a long breathing space in the late forties and fifties before it bubbled up to the surface again.

If one looks at the sort of crimes reported, many of them were the usual things that happened in peacetime, but characterized by a wartime setting or encouraged by war conditions: "Pensioner robbed of £100 in shelter: While he was asleep in a Plymouth air-raid shelter an old-age pensioner was attacked and robbed of £100 which he carried in a body belt. That was the story told at Devon Assizes when X, 22, was sentenced to three years' penal servitude and ordered to receive twelve strokes of the birch." Or the following, which was doubtless exacerbated by the war, but which could happen at any time: "Acting Corporal Y, of the Royal Army Medical Corps, who missed an overseas draft because his wife wanted him to stay in England until their baby was born, has been released from military detention, it was announced in Aldershot. Y's sentence of six months' detention has been suspended."

Certain crimes seem to have been the direct outcome of the war, and are worth closer consideration, especially since *crime passionel*, for example, has never enjoyed the kind of popularity in England that it has had in some other European countries. A, a forty-six years old Civil Servant, was found guilty of the murder of B, a NAAFI canteen manager. A was sentenced to death. The jury added a strong recommendation to mercy, however, in the circumstances. B had been found dead in the bedroom of an Exeter hotel with six bullet wounds in his body. Witnesses told the story of B's association with A's wife, who left her husband on August 20th. For hours he tried to find her. Finally, he arrived at the hotel, went to B's bedroom and shot him with a service revolver which he had obtained, it was stated, by saying that he was a Home Guard instructor. A said he went to the hotel for the purpose of appealing to B: "I asked him to give me a break and not ruin my life and my wife's life, but he laughed and said 'You can have your wife back when I have finished with her.'" That was the last thing he remembered. For the defence it was stated that B's remark, a contemptuous reference to someone A adored, deprived A of his self-control. But the *crime passionel* has never been recognized in Britain, as the judge pointed out. This is only one example, coldly recorded, and yet it must have been the tragedy of many couples during the war, and a source of constant anxiety of husbands and lovers away from home – and wives at home, too.

Problems with evacuees, although often similar to those arising in any conflict between employer and employee, were a direct result of the war in many cases: "An outburst of applause at Derby Assizes last week when the jury found a fifteen years old Manchester boy Not Guilty of the manslaughter of Z, fifty-eight years old farmer . . . brought a rebuke from Mr. Justice Stable." The boy had been billeted on the farmer with his younger brother since the beginning of the war. He was alleged to have hit the farmer on the side of his head with a hoe. The pathologist called to give evidence for the prosecution said that the blow was in itself insufficient to cause death. What probably happened was that the farmer fell awkwardly and struck his head on the ground. In statements to the police the boy said that he had been unhappy and wanted to leave the farm, since Z continually grumbled and swore at him. The farmer, it was stated, was a drunkard, and the boy was his only helper on a farm of 170 acres.

Would the people in court have clapped in peacetime? It is a moot point, and might depend on the way the case had been handled by the Press. But one detects a slight shift of optic, an adjustment of the lens through which people viewed things, not in any conscious way, but in spite of themselves. One story which leaves a particularly bad taste in the mouth is that told by Constantine Fitzgibbon in his book on the Blitz. After a bomb fell on the Café de Paris in London, one of the injured women thought that the fumbling hand she felt amidst the dust and the debris was that of a rescuer, but found to her amazement that it was a thief removing her rings. It is the speed with which the thief arrived on the scene which makes the story more shocking.

More important, the foundations of our democratic society were not affected. Initially the issue of Identity Cards, for example, must have seemed a monstrous imposition to a country unused to them. Even today, one only has to suggest that some similar practice should be introduced – for example, that the nation should have its fingerprints taken – for there to be an enormous outcry. But if one has lived in a country on the verge of civil war, as France was in the late fifties, where groups of armed soldiers stood on every street corner in the capital, and people were liable to be held without adequate explanation, as they may still, then the matter has a different perspective.

A rather vicious attack on the British police appeared in *The Tatler* at the beginning of September, 1940. It seemed rather unnecessary, considering how overworked the British police force was, and the fact that they were never armed, even when invasion seemed imminent. Or perhaps the article was simply the result of someone's hurt feelings? "While nations clash in mortal combat and the whole earth reels under the flame and blood of cosmic conflict, the London police go quietly and conscientiously about their duties of running people in whose dogs cause a 'nuisance' on the pavement and of making quite sure that all night clubs are conducted on strictly Sunday School lines or else shut down . . . . The police can chase the night clubs and bottle parties and the dog owners, but air raid problems just leave them cold. They are not interested. Surely the case is good for a demand for a further increase in the size of an already enormous force which can always find work of a perfectly useless kind for idle hands to do!"

This was just before the beginning of the Blitz, so it is only fair to point out that the tune might well have changed within a matter of days. But freedom and democracy were never at risk from any internal developments. On the contrary, the war gave immense impetus to the evolution of democratic and social forces, and the foundations were laid for many liberal projects. We now seem to be witnessing the erosion of one of the greatest, the Welfare State, and others to our shame have never been completed. A new spirit was abroad. One saw it in the army, encouraged – or some would say fomented – by *The Daily Mirror*.

The army itself was subject to the heave and swell of social change. This was not to the liking of some officers. One intrepid officer went so far as to publish a letter in *The Times* of 15th January, 1941, lamenting the fact that middle, lower middle and working classes were receiving the King's Commission. He was duly sacked, but he certainly represented a type who had a strong hand in the conduct of affairs and against whom *The Daily Mirror* was busy campaigning. This was less true of officers in the Royal Air Force, and in the army the emergence of General Montgomery was extremely important in this respect. However extreme he may have become subsequently, Montgomery's own words about the relations between a general and his men must be seen in the context of their time: "They [the men] want to know what is going on, and what the general wants them to do, and why, and when; they want to see and decide in their own minds what sort of person he is. I have never believed in dealing with soldiers by a process of 'remote control'; they are human beings and their lives are precious."

George Orwell, in *The Lion and the Unicorn*, saw the war totally in political and social terms: "If we can survive this war, the defeat in Flanders will turn out to have been one of the great turning points in English history. In that spectacular disaster the working class, the middle class and even a section of the business community could see the utter rottenness of private capitalism. For the first time in their lives, the comfortable were uncomfortable, the professional optimists had to admit that there was something wrong."

For a view from someone who would no doubt be classified as belonging to the "other side", but who saw himself caught between the two, one finds the following in Harold Nicolson's diary for January, 1940, where he speaks of ". . . the great and angry tide which is rising against the governing classes. I have always been on the side of the under-dog, but I have also believed in the principle of aristocracy. I have hated the rich but I have loved learning, scholarship, intelligence and the humanities. Suddenly I am faced with the fact that all these lovely things are supposed to be 'class privileges' . . .".

A rather Olympian statement, which became a kind of gospel for leftish liberals, was published by *The Times* on 1st July, 1940: "If we speak of democracy, we do not mean a democracy which maintains the right to vote but forgets the right to work and the right to live. If we speak of freedom, we do not mean a rugged individualism which excludes social organization and economic planning. If we speak of equality, we do not mean political equality nullified by social and economic privilege. If we speak of economic reconstruction, we think less of maximum production (though this too will be required) than of equitable distribution . . . . The European house cannot be put in order unless we put our own house in order first. The new order cannot be based on the preservation of privilege, whether the privilege be that of a country, of a class, or of an individual."

Brave words, which would nowadays be applauded by most people. Unfortunately the reality is different. Nevertheless as far as the life of the people of Britain is concerned, the war established or affirmed certain social principles. Whether we retreat from ground already gained, or fail to achieve the heights we would like to scale, we can never escape from the fact that those principles were affirmed.

The National Health Service is an example of the first. An enormous amount of ground has been gained, but we now seem to be in retreat, not for ideological reasons, but for economic reasons. As early as 1930 the British Medical Association had put forward the idea of "A General Medical Service for the Nation" and this was revised in 1938, after three intermediate reports on Scotland in 1936, Britain in 1937 and the Sankey Report of 1937. In October, 1941, the Minister of Health announced in the House of Commons that "It is the objective of the government so soon as may be after the war to ensure that by means of a comprehensive hospital service appropriate treatment shall be readily available to every person in need of it."

The Beveridge Report of November, 1942, was to state unequivocally that the report itself must rest on the assumption that there would be a Health Service which would ". . . ensure that for every citizen there is available whatever treatment he requires in whatever form he requires it . . .". Finally, on 18th February, 1944, the government produced its White Paper, "A National Health Service." The bill was subsequently presented to Parliament on 19th March, 1946.

It is not really surprising that the Labour Party should have been returned to power after the war. Churchill must have realised why, though he chose to put it in terms which sound striking but present a very selective view of the facts of the situation: ". . . at the outset of this mighty battle, I acquired the chief power in the State, which henceforth I wielded in ever-growing measure for five years and three months of world war, at the end of which time, all our enemies having surrendered unconditionally or being about to do so, I was immediately dismissed by the British electorate from all further conduct of their affairs."

This was not so, for he returned to head another government when the nation had grown sick of Attlee's austerity and post-war socialism. But the men and women who returned home to England in 1945 from the battlefields abroad, and the nation at home which had outlived its finest hour, wanted not military honour but social equality, not world prestige (though probably still taking this for granted) but material prosperity. Those battles have still not been won, as far as certain sections of the community are concerned, and we have seen the battle for material prosperity turn into a headlong rush of acquisitiveness.

In all fairness to Winston Churchill, however, he never forgot that the House of Commons was the supreme authority in the land, although there were times when he seemed to ignore it. There were occasions, for example, when he seemed to identify himself with his great forebear the Duke of Marlborough, and he seems to have remembered too late – certainly in the passage quoted above – that the nation he led was in fact an electorate, and not a flock committed to his care by divine providence.

6. The Human Story

" . . . Just to let you know we are quite safe and
well, only a bit shaken.

"We had a terrible attack about 9.30 pm just
going to put up our beds on the ground floor when the
house trembled . . ."

London mother to her son, 19 September 1940

On 7th September, 1940, towards the end of the afternoon, London received its first real taste of the Blitz and its heaviest daylight raid of the war. Although the Germans bombed suburbs as far apart as Tottenham in the north and Croydon in the south, and up river from Woolwich to Westminster and beyond, the full force of the attack fell on London's East End. The docks and Woolwich Arsenal were the objectives, but it was inevitable that the densely populated riverside boroughs of West Ham, Poplar, Stepney and Bermondsey should also suffer heavily. These were the boroughs least equipped to cope with the destruction, and so vicious was the first onslaught that many people imagined it to be the long-awaited knock-out blow. The German planes returned in the evening hours and kept up the bombardment until the following morning. They came back again that Sunday evening, and on the following nights, and it was not until Wednesday, 11th September, that London's anti-aircraft barrage answered back. The barrage was not in a position to return much damage, but its contribution to popular morale was enormous. People cheered in the streets when they heard the guns.

Although 842 people were killed on these first two nights, and well over 2,000 seriously injured, a feeling of relief flooded over many sections of the community that at last it had happened; the unknown had revealed itself. This was no comfort whatsoever for the bereaved and the homeless, the maimed and the dispossessed, but for the country at large and Londoners in particular, they were at last seeing action.

The tragedy was that such a shock was needed to spur some people into activity, when more preparation might have avoided loss of life and injury on such a large scale. A further tragedy, particularly as far as provincial towns were concerned, was that those responsible for their defence seem to have learned nothing from

Their Finest Hour

London's experience – initially, at any rate – so that when Coventry was attacked in November and even the following spring, when Plymouth was raided, the local authorities were almost unable to cope. The bombing of Rotterdam on 14th May, 1940, should have given some warning of what England might expect, but details were kept from the public as far as possible. In his speeches Winston Churchill made only the broadest of references to it, so that although an overall picture of disaster was put across, the real horror was played down. The local authorities should have been more aware, through government directives, what to expect and what measures to take. However, the government's machinery for handing out such directives was deficient, and in any case unrestrained publicity of such horrors might have had a disastrous effect on morale. In view of Britain's shaky defences, morale was a crucial weapon in the armoury. But people were not easily fooled: when they had lived through raids and picked up the newspapers next day to read about what had happened, but found only a short paragraph or footnote, they were at first either puzzled or irritated. But in the end they accepted the censorship as a convention.

People were usually willing to accept such restrictions once the bombing began because, as Lord Boothby has said, after months of anticipation there was a kind of white hot flame which Winston Churchill ignited. But leaving aside the star performers, we shall see how it all appeared to Michael Stapleton, who lived and worked in Hackney and Islington throughout the Blitz:

> If I heard an aeroplane I used to rush out as quickly as I could either into the garden or into the street or over to Hackney Downs, and wait for something to happen. We had an absolute ache for something to happen. We had a desperately phoney sort of war as far as we could tell, in which we had earned no credit, none at all, and suddenly things were beginning to happen. But there was the strange hiatus from the time that Hitler occupied the Channel ports and the Blitz really getting under way. There was this terrible sort of in-between time when nothing, even so, seemed to be happening, and we desperately wanted something to happen. To me, at the age of seventeen, it represented some sort of excitement at least. I wasn't thinking about bombs falling on me, but I think that when you're seventeen you never do.
>
> At the time of the Battle of Britain and the beginning of the Blitz I was working in a butcher's shop in Islington – John Street – which is a street that leads into Chapel Street Market. I knew the market very well. We had had air-raid warnings – several of them – which had come to nothing. I remember being very keyed up by those warnings, thinking that something was about to happen. I don't think I ever consciously thought that something must happen, but I think a lot of people had that feeling, and on that particular Saturday afternoon I was

busy about my usual butcher's-boy job which, on a Saturday afternoon, was to scrub down all the woodwork. It being fine weather, it was always simpler to yank all the things out onto the pavement and scrub them there. I was doing that, and there was a branch of a big department store just on the corner. I remember nodding to the counter-hands who worked in there and who came and went. Then at one point there seemed to be an awful lot of aircraft about, and I couldn't remember if the warning had gone or not. I said to somebody "Is there a warning on?" The person I asked simply nodded and went on. So I began to look at the sky and then I found that other people were looking at the sky. We began to hear a lot of noise from I wasn't quite sure where, but it later proved to be in the dockland area.

It was getting on for late afternoon – half-past four, towards five – and we began to see aircraft buzzing about in the sky, a perfect sky – it was the most perfect autumn, the autumn of the Blitz. A lot of people were out by this time, watching the sky, and I don't quite remember at what point what seemed to be isolated aircraft flying in towards us became suddenly a great black mass, a formation flight – of bombers. There seemed to me to be about twelve in each squadron and they simply followed each other in waves of twelve.

Into the middle of it dived the Spitfires and the Hurricanes and there seemed to be so few, almost like three or four flies attacking a huge, big black beetle wearing a carapace of armour. They could seem to have no effect on them as far as we could see, but they were "ours" and of course everybody was rooting for them like mad. It didn't yield or break up immediately but we did see that at some part of this tangle of machinery, thousands of feet up in the sky, at one point, two or three figures floated down on the end of parachutes. First we assumed that they were Germans, and then it occurred to us – the way it does to a group of people when one of them voices it – that they could as easily be Spitfire or Hurricane pilots.

We watched them with fascinated interest drifting down, wondering where they were drifting down to, and the wave of aircraft had passed out of sight by this time – from where we were standing – which was at the Angel in Islington. Of course all this took about twenty minutes. It seemed to me that we had been standing there for hours. We began to see that there was smoke rising from the East. Work had to be done, nevertheless – that was one of the strange things about the Blitz, that work had to be done anyway, no matter what was happening outside, you couldn't put down your work and go out and look at it.

We had all gone back inside to carry on with the business of closing up the shop on a Saturday afternoon, when somebody came in and said " They've got the Docks. You can see the smoke from here." So of course we all poured back out into the street and looked over towards the East, moving up towards Pentonville Road – that gives you a fairly clear view right down City Road into the City and into the East, and there were thick columns of smoke rising from there.

Well, the time came for us shutting up, and we didn't waste any time over that. We shut up shop quick and we all departed and went our different ways. I got on my bike and went back to Hackney and wondered what was going to happen next. I thought I'd see a film, which was what I usually did on a Saturday night. Then my brother came home and he didn't seem to know very much about it because he worked in Hackney and was that much farther removed from it. In some strange way it was an aimless sort of evening, for suddenly an element of uncertainty had come in when what had been before had been routine. You just went on with your own life. When night fell my brother said to me "Do you suppose we had better go into the shelter?" I said "Well, I suppose we'd better." The family upstairs were already leaving to go into the shelter. There was a small baby, husband and wife, and there was a man on the top floor whose wife and child were evacuated. We saw them making their way down the garden towards the Anderson and we thought, well, perhaps we had better.

So we joined them, and it was rather horrible – terribly close and stuffy – and I wasn't liking it at all. As soon as it was completely dark the raids began – or the raid of that night began. For the first time I experienced bombs falling near enough to shake the Anderson – you know, to really make the ground move under me. We heard them in the distance and we knew that it was mainly in the East because that was where the noise was coming from, and where we could see flames and smoke. Where we were, which was more or less off the main line; if they were coming in from the South-east we were just a little too far off that, to the West of the main track, we thought, to get the brunt of it that night. Of course we didn't realise that that night they were particularly aiming at the dockland area.

So we talked and talked, and occasionally we all stopped talking and listened, and then we went on talking. The married couple were doing their best with their baby, who was very unhappy and fretful at being in this strange place, not knowing quite why. It was impossible not to keep going out of the shelter. We were in and out of the shelter looking at nothing very much because it was all happening too far away. Towards midnight we drifted back in and spread ourselves out on the floor of the shelter. We had floored it, as a matter of fact. I had an old overcoat and slept in that, and it seemed to me we had been silent and asleep for about ten minutes when we heard the first bombs falling in the vicinity, in our neighbourhood.

The noise of the bombs is quite indescribable. It's not a scream. It's not the way people tell it, a lot of the time, who didn't hear it, that bombs fall with a scream that increases and then suddenly cuts out. It doesn't sound like that at all. It sounds like gravel on a corrugated-iron roof – very, very fine gravel – that increases, the noise increases, as the bomb comes down. As it comes whooshing through the air, and that noise gets louder and louder, then there's the split second when that stops and the next moment you're literally holding onto anything that will hold you upright or give you something to cling to. It took me completely by surprise because I was simply lying flat on my back on the floor of the shelter – and I heard this, and there wasn't anything I could have done, and I didn't think of doing anything. I heard it in a completely detached way. Then they came in quick succession, three or four of them, one after the other. Earth rained in through the cracks. The baby woke up screaming, poor little thing, and the married couple were of course consoling the baby and each other, and the man whose wife and child were evacuated said something like 'Bastards!' That was all he said. Then we settled down again and waited for daylight. I don't think any of us slept.

Daylight came fairly early. It was September. As soon as it was daylight I scrambled out and looked around. I couldn't see any smouldering ruins or anything and I climbed onto the wall and looked over the Downs and there was no sign of it there. I didn't feel like going out and investigating or walking round. I walked back down the garden path to the house and found that we didn't possess a single window. Not one. There were sheets of glass everywhere. All four floors. And I walked straight into it without knowing it. Straight into it. I looked around because I heard something, and it was my brother who had followed me down and said 'How do we keep the draught out?'

We went in and made some tea, and then we went back and everybody was, by this time, scrambling out. We had been going to ask them if they would like a cup of tea but they were all plainly going into their own flats anyway, so we didn't bother. Most of the morning was spent in clearing away the broken glass and picking up things that had been knocked down, inside the flat. My father was away that night, I remember, because he had a lady he was courting. He was a widower and was courting a lady who lived at Chingford. So he wasn't there. He came home about half-past nine or ten and surveyed all this wreckage with dismay and then began to be very sergeant-majorish, hectoring and ordering about getting things that we could put over the windows to keep out the draught and keep out the air. So most of Sunday was spent doing that.

We hadn't thought of plastering our windows with strips. A lot of people did though, and did it very conscientiously. A great many shopkeepers had wooden shutters over their windows – built on – which was a very good idea. Mind, if the blast had been sufficient it wouldn't have made any difference. It would have smashed them anyway.

You just got whatever you could to block up the windows. You searched in the cellar, you searched around the few bits of timber you had in the garden. You tried to find those, and if you couldn't you made a thin frame and nailed lino onto it, and that was how you did it. That was all you could use, there was nothing else. Lino was a great favourite, I remember that. If you were lucky enough to have wood then you just boarded up the window, or you boarded up the two sides of the frame, so that you were at least able to lift the sash bar to open it and let some light in, but in the winter you were likely to spend a lot of time in the dark.

That Sunday we had another air-raid warning which lasted all night, but I can't remember that anything sensational happened. But that was the beginning of it, and after that we settled down to the Blitz. It seemed that in no time at all air raids were happening, on and off, all day; to the point where, when you heard the sound of the siren, you listened to find out whether there was an air raid on or whether there was not one on. You got so confused.

After that, life began to take on a pattern which was new and strange at first, but people soon got used to it. People were suddenly living in the present in a way that most of them had never experienced in their lives before.

During the day, looking through the shop window in the middle of some job or other, I'd hear the siren go and the next thing would see frantic mothers running, pushing their prams in front of them, to the nearest shelter. I'm sure they were thinking of their children. Night after night people got their bit of bedding or whatever it was, and they all trooped into the shelters. They trooped down into the underground stations. It's impossible to visualise unless you saw it, but the platforms of every single underground station were lined by bunks. Not at first. At first you simply went down and lay on the concrete and slept on it if you could. How people could sleep in those conditions baffled me.

It might be wondered that nobody stopped and thought "How long is this going on?" I'm sure nobody did. Speaking for myself, I never did. From my own point of view, shelters became an abomination. My father went to the Anderson shelter regularly, and was very insistent that my brother and myself would go as well, but we hated it. They were astonishingly successful things because they were only corrugated iron, and it was very simple to erect them. You just piled the earth on them. If you were on dry ground, that is. If you weren't, then it was hard luck, because you just stepped into two feet of water, quite easily, and it had to be emptied every morning. What happened to the people who got those – I don't know how they managed.

After the first week I refused point blank to go near a shelter. I remember having a raging row with my father over this very thing. I used simply to go to bed, and take my chance. Living in a basement flat, of course, I was – to a certain extent – sitting pretty. But a lot of people who weren't took the same point of view that I did. They used to go home and go to bed because they knew that if they did, they were taking a chance and they might never see the next day. On the other hand, if they went into a shelter the same thing might happen, and they would be in miserable discomfort. Of course you could not blame people with children for taking them to shelters. Obviously they would have to do that.

There were all kinds of shelters. There were the shelters in the parks – long, long tunnels. They were awful. When you went in there the smell of cigarettes and humanity and people packed close together – people who, with the best will in the world couldn't get a bath a lot of the time, and a lot of the time didn't have a bath. There weren't baths in houses in East London. That was grim. The underground wasn't quite as bad – at least it was warm. Howling draughts used to blow through, but generally it wasn't a cold place.

The shelters that I remember most vividly were in a huge block of council flats across the road. These were sub-surface shelters. They weren't quite underground. There was a sort of area of them which was just above ground and had ventilation grilles. I think they were called surface shelters, with reinforced concrete tops. I remember a particularly nasty night when there was a direct hit on one of them. I thought the house had been hit. I jumped up in bed and called out to my brother. He said "It must be across the road." We dressed and rushed out. It was a very dark night. You couldn't see anything, but you could hear screaming. There was a great pall of dust over everything. There were the ambulances arriving. As the dust cleared and you could see a bit, you got used to the light and the ambulance men's torches. It was unbelievable. The carnage was quite frightful. I remember lifting a great block of concrete off one man and finding that there wasn't any of him under it except the part that I could see.

This was how London came into the front line of battle. This was how a seventeen-year old boy came face to face with war and death. Catastrophe fitted into the normal routine of life – or the normal routine of life bravely asserted itself in the face of catastrophe.

There was a street called Risinghill Street, and I remember that there a land mine struck, and Risinghill Street was absolutely demolished. It was simply flattened. I used to go through there delivering with my roundsman's bike. Even at that time – strange as it may seem – one could still be delivering meat to catering orders, which were on a different rationing basis, and I delivered to several of the pubs in the King's Cross area which did meals. I often went on the side streets because there were tram tracks on Pentonville Road, and that was a very nasty way to go on a wet day. You could get your wheels involved in tram tracks. It wasn't funny to go flying sideways off the bike when you had a basketful of meat.

I decided on this particular day that I would go down through Risinghill Street and join Pentonville Road much farther down, but I wasn't allowed access. I was turned away. I saw them carrying a long procession of bodies on stretchers, carrying them out of shelters. You were involved in voluntary rescue work at almost any time – involuntarily you were involved. It was the cloud of dust that told you something had happened. Very often there wasn't any flame, and you just joined in and did what you could. My father was at this time involved in a stretcher party. He was on a strange shift. They were on for twenty-four hours and off for twenty-four hours, but they could be called out at any time.

In fact the twenty-four hour shift had the advantage that people did not have to travel backwards and forwards during raids at night or in the early morning, when they were exposed to all sorts of dangers and the business of picking one's way through bombed or blazing streets was doubly difficult.

Although the London Blitz kept up virtually non-stop until the beginning of November, 1940, and then at a slightly less concentrated rate until May, 1941, during late October the Germans began to turn to the provinces, and on the 25th of that month 170 people died in Birmingham. But it was Coventry which really marked the transition, when it was attacked on 14th November. The Germans were now using a pathfinder group who located their target with the help of radio beams and then set it ablaze with incendiaries. The bombers then followed and simply dropped their load into the conflagration. More than 500 tons of bombs were dropped. The attack opened early in the evening and lasted ten hours. 554 people were killed and 865 seriously injured. Almost one third of Coventry's houses were either destroyed or so damaged as to be virtually uninhabitable. Six out of seven telephone lines were put out of action; the railway lines were blocked, and the centre of the city, with its medieval streets and beautiful cathedral, was laid waste. *Gone with the Wind* had opened that evening at one of the city's cinemas and had ended at 10.30 p.m. At 11 p.m. the cinema was a smoking ruin. A year passed before the film came back to Coventry. Water, gas and electricity supplies were almost non-existent. Water carts had to be brought round daily but people went into neighbouring towns and villages to fill pots and pans with water. Rationing had to be abandoned, and there were outbreaks of hysteria of the kind predicted on a large scale before war broke out.

It is perhaps surprising that the horror of Coventry did not happen earlier. The city was vital to the British war economy and represented an obvious military target. But comfort had been taken in the fact that it lay in a hollow and was usually hidden by a pall of smoke and pollution. It was later revealed that the German pilots had been told to bomb only industrial targets, but in fact about a hundred acres of the city centre were devastated. A new German word was coined – *Coventrieren*, to "Coventrate".

Hollow or no hollow, smoke pall or no smoke pall, the British authorities must surely have realized that Coventry was an obvious target. Yet the city's method of coping with the disaster was no better than that of London at the beginning of September. Indeed, because Coventry was organically a more united community than London, the effect of the raid on the inhabitants was so much more shattering. They could not call on the resources of neighbouring boroughs, or go to the shops in the nearest high street, of which there are many in London. When the centre of Coventry was paralysed, the city was paralysed. Miraculously industry was not brought to a standstill. Production was damaged for six to eight weeks, and the normal life of the city was seriously disrupted. But such was the determination of the people that five out of six went to work in the first week after the raid, and in a space of only six weeks, production in some factories was back to what it had been before the raid.

Another heavy raid on Coventry took place in April of the following year, in which up to 250 German bombers were involved. Casualties were similarly heavy. Although it can have been no compensation for the citizens of Coventry, their ordeal of 14th November at least prepared them for the next bombing and forced the army to be involved in a new way. The War Office had envisaged a certain involvement of the military before the November Coventry raid, but its role was seen as a guardian of law and order. After the raid the troops took part in clearing up the city and making good the damage.

The biggest single area of war devastation in all Britain was created by the great City of London fire of 29th December, 1940. Many buildings had no fire watchers and were locked up for the Christmas vacation. The water failed because of a burst main, and the River Thames was at a very low ebb. Miraculously St. Paul's Cathedral survived the conflagration, though at one moment it seemed so certain that it must go that a newspaper correspondent cabled across the Atlantic to that effect. Michael Stapleton witnessed the event without realizing at first what was going on:

"When I came out of the cinema there was a raid in progress. I looked East

F

along Long Acre and saw a great red flare in the sky. I didn't know what it was. I went on towards Piccadilly and then something made me turn back. I walked to Charing Cross and looked back along the Strand. There was no mistaking it, something was burning, and burning pretty fiercely. There was a huge fire in the East. While I was looking some more bombs started falling.

"I walked down Shaftesbury Avenue towards Holborn, and the fire seemed to get brighter and brighter, through the rain, and I tried to work out where I was looking, and it seemed to me that I was looking towards St. Paul's and Smithfield – that area. I came to the Angel and turned round by Sadler's Wells and looked down St. John's Street and there it was really very red indeed. It was quite the biggest fire that I had remembered, and I stood there watching it. I spoke to another bystander and asked him what it was.

"The next morning, when I went to work, one of the first jobs I had was to take the bike down to Smithfield Market and get some seasoning there. I got as far as the market and found that you couldn't go anywhere. The whole of that part of London seemed to be sealed off. There were still flickers of flames. There were fire engines everywhere. You couldn't cross a road without picking your way across hosepipes. There were great black masses floating about, ash and soot, around St. Paul's. I left the bike and walked through the market and at one point was ordered back, so I said, 'I've got to go through; this is the way I came,' and went on walking. I was just being nosey. I should have had something better to do. Everything seemed to be the result of a fire. Everything seemed to have been burned or bombed or in some way damaged. There was water everywhere. Water was just pouring everywhere from the fire engines that had been at work. That was the 'Night of the Fire' for most of us. That was how we remembered it. The night when they set fire to the City of London. I didn't know what had happened until afterwards, when I read about it."

London was big enough to absorb such raids. Within its boundaries it contained the biggest single area of war devastation in the country caused by the City fire, and parts of West Ham were so flattened that the army used the area for training in street fighting. In the smaller provincial towns, raids like that were far more effective.

A similar raid to the Coventry one was that on Clydebank, near Glasgow, on 13th and 14th March, 1941, and also the one at Plymouth on 20th and 21st March. The Plymouth raid is worth looking at in some detail, since it was yet another provincial centre of strategic importance, and more than six months had elapsed since the beginning of the Blitz on London. On 20th March King George and Queen Elizabeth visited Plymouth. It was a happy day, with an atmosphere of festivity that was becoming rarer as the months went by. There was music, and dancing on Plymouth Hoe. Soon after the royal party left, the first of the German planes began to arrive and the bombs began to fall. German records show that 155 planes took part on the first night and 168 on the second. Naval and military installations suffered little damage, but the whole of the centre of the city within a 600-yard radius of the Guildhall was razed to the ground. The water supply failed and most of the shopping centre was destroyed by fire. On the two nights of the raid more than 18,000 houses were destroyed or damaged, 329 people died and 283 were seriously injured. Some 5,000 people were made homeless. Once more, almost six months after the Blitz on London had begun, post-raid services in a provincial centre – including one which should have been regarded as a prime target – were completely inadequate.

A month later, Plymouth was again the target. It really seemed as if the Germans were out to annihilate it. On 21st, 22nd and 23rd April, and again on 28th and 29th, between 100 and 150 planes bombed the city each night without let up. Almost 600 people died and 440 were seriously wounded. A further 20,000 houses were damaged, and what there was left of the shopping centre was obliterated. This time the dockyard was not spared. In his book *Only the Stars are Neutral*, Quintin Reynolds, who had lived through the London Blitz, and seen war-damaged Coventry, Southampton and Liverpool, wrote: "nothing I had seen prepared me for the sight of Plymouth." A large-scale operation had to be mounted to save the city from complete collapse. Some 40,000 people were now homeless, food supplies were down to a tenth of their usual capacity. Had the Germans pressed the attack, the total evacuation of the civilian population might have been necessary.

Plymouth showed very well why it was that a sprawling urban area the size of London could absorb raids of great severity, and yet not receive the knock-out blow, whereas a city like Plymouth, with the sea in front of it and a very rural and thinly populated hinterland, took a similar raid very badly indeed. Once the Blitz got under way in London there was less and less mention of the knock-out blow, as Londoners began to realize that "we can take it". But Plymouth, for example – its own lack of preparation apart – could not call for help from any neighbouring boroughs; its refugees had only the empty hillsides to flee to.

In some respects, however, the worst was yet to come for London itself. It saw the last, and arguably the worst, raid of this phase of the Blitz on 10th May. No less than 1,450 people perished; many of London's famous landmarks were hit – Westminster Abbey, the Tower of London and the House of Commons among them. The Conservative M.P. Sir Henry Channon returned from the country: "I left the lovely May countryside with regret and drove up to London; where I found burnt bits of paper fluttering about in the street, and broken glass everywhere. The rubble and debris are heaped high in the streets. I tried to get to the

House of Commons but the crowd was so large I could not fight my way through; but I could see the huge hole in the Westminster Hall roof. I met Jim Thomas who tells me that the Chamber is gutted: no more shall we hear fiery and futile speeches there . . . gone is that place, as I always foresaw. Itself the cradle, the protector of democracy in the end it went a long way to kill what it created . . .".

Channon's panegyric seems a little effusive for what was, after all, a fairly recent Victorian creation, and he was wrong about there being no more speeches. There have been many – fiery and futile – since its restoration. But obviously the bombing was a very emotional thing, and deeply saddened many members of the House. Winston Churchill is said to have wept when he surveyed the ruins. Harold Nicolson recorded this impression in his diary: "I go to see the ruins of the old Chamber. It is impossible to get through the Members' Lobby which is a mass of twisted girders. So I went up by the staircase to the Ladies' Gallery and then suddenly, when I turned the corridor, there was the open air and a sort of Tintern Abbey gaping before me. The little Ministers' rooms to right and left of the Speaker's Lobby were still intact, but from there onwards there was absolutely nothing."

The reference to Tintern Abbey is an interesting one, because in his poem, Wordsworth expressed what many people must have felt about the coming of war; about their past life, which many thought had gone for ever, and the general human condition:

> ". . . That time is past,
> And all its aching joys are now no more,
> And all its dizzy raptures. Not for this
> Faint I, nor mourn nor murmur; other gifts
> Have followed; for such loss, I would believe,
> Abundant recompense. For I have learned
> To look on nature, not as in the hour
> Of thoughtless youth; but hearing oftentimes
> The still, sad music of humanity . . .".

Between September, 1940, and May, 1941, 90,000 casualties were suffered in London, of whom 20,000 were killed and 25,000 seriously injured. The figures for Britain as a whole during 1940 and 1941 were 43,000 deaths from bombs; another 17,000 civilians were to die in the rest of the war. Roughly half of all those deaths were in London. By way of comparison, 285,691 members of the forces lost their lives in the war. According to expert calculations made before the war concerning the effect of bombing, the 18,000 tons of bombs dropped on London alone during the Blitz would have accounted for all the forces' wartime deaths. And yet, if disaster was expected on such a vast scale, why was there not more preparation?

How could the authorities possibly have coped if the figures were anywhere near what had been expected? On 30th September, 1940, several Londoners who had lost their homes in the East End were told to go to the Victoria Palace in the Mile End Road where arrangements would be made for them to be rehoused and compensated for war damage. At the Victoria Palace they were to fill in a form, but the supply of forms had run out. They were then asked to leave their addresses so that forms could be sent to them – which was, of course, precisely why they were there: they no longer had addresses.

Churchill typically described the period of the war which followed on from the Battle of Britain in this way: "After shooting Niagara we now had had to struggle in the rapids." Angus Calder, in his book *The People's War*, puts his finger quite clearly on the change in the overall situation which took place between 1940 and 1941: "In the blitzed cities, it was a hectic period of courage and improvisation; but even as the blitz proceeded, what might be called the 'amateur' war was coming to an end. 1941 was the year in which the war economy emerged in something close to its final vigour; the year when shortages of food and consumer goods began to become oppressive; when the recruitment of women for the war effort was taken in hand; when the workers in the factories and in Civil Defence were subjected to compulsion; when political sourness re-entered the organs of public opinion. 1940 had been the year of individual efforts coalescing in desperate activities; 1941 was the year in which the Central Statistical Office was formed as part of the War Cabinet secretariat, the year in which Government departments began in earnest to redress their lack of knowledge of Britain's economic units of production, sale and consumption, and to reduce such activities to neat tables of numbers."

In other words, the end of their finest hour came not with a bang, but with neat tables of numbers. One Londoner in six, some 1,400,000 people, had been made homeless at one time or another by the end of May, 1941, and in the borough of Stepney four out of ten houses had been destroyed or damaged as early as 11th November, 1940. So the statistics roll on. One can easily lose sight of the human factor after a while, and the impersonal official reports published soon after the war emphasize this tendency.

But there are some human factors which were not necessarily apparent, even to fairly perceptive people, at the time. One of these phenomena was the way in which people came together, quite of their own accord, in the circumstances of war. In some cases this comradeship ended almost as abruptly as it had begun when the crisis was over, but this above all things seems to have made the war such an exhilarating experience for many people. It was, after all, the most exciting thing that ever happened, or is likely to have happened, to millions of people – death and destruction apart – and they now remember it as a time of great friendliness, activity, solidarity and trust. Many long to recapture that spirit now, but somehow it eludes them. It is sad to think that something on the scale of a national disaster would be needed to recreate it.

In her novel *The Heat of the Day*, Elizabeth Bowen has given us a fine and memorable poetic statement of what people thought and felt, and the physical quality of life: "The night behind and the night to come met across every noon in an arch of strain. To work or think was to ache. In offices, factories, ministries, shops, kitchens the hot yellow sands of each afternoon ran out slowly; fatigue was the one reality. You dared not envisage sleep. Apathetic, the injured and dying in the hospitals watched the light change on walls which might fall tonight. Those rendered homeless sat where they had been sent; or, worse, with the obstinacy of animals retraced their steps to look for what was no longer there. Most of all the dead, from mortuaries, from under cataracts of rubble, made their anonymous presence – not as today's dead but as yesterday's living – felt through London.

"These unknown dead reproached those left living by their unknownness, which could not be mended now. Who had the right to mourn them, not having cared that they had lived? So, among the crowds still eating, drinking, working, travelling, halting, there began to be an instinctive movement to break down indifference while there was still time. The wall between the living and the living became less solid as the wall between the living and the dead thinned."

7. Life Goes On

"There'll be bluebirds over
The white cliffs of Dover,
Tomorrow, just you wait and see . . .".
                    Words of a popular song

As we have seen, a striking feature of wartime life was the way in which people adapted to circumstances, and the way in which crisis became a cohesive force. An elderly lady wrote in a letter a week after the London Blitz: "We are most fortunate – for the noise and huge gunfire are the worst we have to bear, especially at night when our beds and house shake." She knew that there were many much worse off than she was. But the phoney war had made people critical and petty minded. As Michael Stapleton put it: "I think people suffered badly from a lack of co-operation. I think they were, to a large extent, bloody minded. It was 'them' and 'us' and it wasn't until the Blitz got under way really seriously that they stopped thinking about 'them' and 'us'. The Auxiliary Fire Service proved itself a hundred times over within the first week . . . but until then they were just another arm of 'them'. The Regulars were very superior in their attitude to them, also."

But in much broader terms, as an immigrant from Ireland, he took a more detached view about the phenomenon: "Life took on a peculiar unreality. It is true, I think, that the English are far better when they are pressed. They really do get together and make a darned good show of it. And whether they are masochistic by nature I don't know, but it always seems to bring out the best in them. As an Irishman, I used to watch this, even then, and wonder about it. Why, when they had everything – for instance in 1938 – there were able-bodied men in their thirties singing in the street just to get enough to eat – why they couldn't manage that, but along came the Blitz and immediately they all adored each other and stood by each other."

They did indeed stand by each other, and it is in this respect that the British people knew their finest hour in 1940. In sharp contrast to this warm desire to help others, to "make do" and carry on, was bureaucracy's seemingly congenital inability to handle what had already been provided for, let alone adapt imaginatively to new developments as ordinary British people were doing each day.

Although by the end of 1941 invasion seemed unlikely – especially after June when Hitler invaded Russia – the thought was still very much in people's minds. It was particularly evident in letters and diaries during May, a month of vicious raids. On 28th December of that year, however, Hugh Cudlipp told how, a few nights earlier, he had read through the secret defence plans for the Isle of Thanet, which was officially regarded as the most likely beachhead for a German invasion. Three vital bridges, supposed to be guarded night and day against parachutists, were to Cudlipp's definite knowledge left unguarded. Civil administration was to be taken over by Colonel ————, in the event of invasion, but the name had never been filled in. Three majors were to taken over the post office, food supply and other services, but of those three officers one was dead and the other two had been posted abroad.

It gives a rather hollow ring to Churchill's fine-sounding phrases in his own book *Their Finest Hour*: "The reader of these pages in future years should realize how dense and baffling is the veil of the Unknown. Now in the full light of the after-time it is easy to see where we were ignorant or too much alarmed, where we were careless or clumsy. . . . He would have been a very foolish man who allowed his reasoning, however clean-cut and seemingly sure, to blot out any possibility against which provision could be made." Considering how "too much alarmed" the experts had been over the danger to the people, then there were remarkably few provisions made or possibilities blotted out.

It had been decided – certainly by August, 1939 – that the London tubes would not be available to shelterers, but the public were not informed of this until after Chamberlain's broadcast on 3rd September. More seriously, shelters were not being produced fast enough. The building of surface shelters was stepped up in consequence, but in the event the public simply took the law into their own hands and used the tubes. Whether the march on the Savoy Hotel from the East End on 15th September, 1940, achieved what its organizers claimed – namely to have forced the government's hand on the deep shelter issue – is still open to debate. Now that the relevant Cabinet papers have been released, strong circumstantial evidence suggests that Mr. Piratin (one of the organizers) is right. To the public at large, however, the whole thing was something of a lead balloon.

People hung on. The lack of sleep began to tell: "People began to look haggard – pale and washed out," said one. And yet they clung to whatever semblance of normality they could, which was a great support at such a time. They also had each other for comfort and encouragement, though too often this new-found comradeship evaporated with the all-clear sirens.

One must remember the amazing work of the Women's Voluntary Service – w.v.s. – which was present almost without exception when anything happened, or wherever need arose. Charles Graves' admirable book *Women in Green*, published in 1948 after the first eight years of the w.v.s., tells the story in full for those who wish to read it. Lady Reading's introduction rightly noted "that for any social service to be of real benefit to the nation as a whole, it must be countrywide in its application, and have territorial coverage. No necessary social service should be allowed to happen sporadically." As she went on to emphasize, the statutory obligation had still to rest with the local government. The need for the w.v.s. arose, however, for this very reason. There was no national framework, to see that local authorities had made at least a minimum of precautions and services on which to draw as a common factor. w.v.s. grew in response to the demands of new situations. As an example of what the w.v.s. did in the field of troop welfare alone, here are extracts from the monthly report sent to headquarters from Malvern at the end of October, 1941:

"1 Found a group of workers willing to undertake all minor repairs to the Belgian Army.

"2 Gave the Italian prisoners of war 25 Jews Harps. They asked for musical instruments and the shops have none. . . .

"5 Stayed a fight between Belgians and Sailors and sent the latter a different way home. . . .

"9 Books sent to Canteen Libraries, lonely outposts, w.r.n.s., *etc.*

"10 Gave a Polish sailor who has no English some picture puzzles. He has a dog. . . .

"20 Mending parties continue to function. . . .

"23 Sent a report to the Home Guard about the formation of an Auxiliary Home Guard in Malvern (no shooting)."

As to the Blitz itself, by the end of the first period, that is May, 1941, 102 members of the w.v.s. had been killed and many more wounded. Five George medals had been awarded and two British Empire medals, but all the individual acts of heroism will never be known.

When the sheer horror and shock of the Blitz had been overcome, one of the most surprising elements, looking back, was the fierce belief in the future – certainly during the latter half of 1941. When it became obvious that the war would not end quickly, many people turned their minds to the future, in a variety of ways. At one end of the scale was the wishful thinking of the advertisement which, in late 1941, read: "When considering your shipbuilding plans for the post-war period, don't forget X of Cowes." At the other was the woman aircraft designer who, when asked what she would design if the world were at peace, said: "I am already on it. A new civil transport machine. That is where the struggle will come after the war." Of course, no shadows were cast by the atomic bomb and a nuclear holocaust in 1941, so there was more cause for hope – or less for pessimism, strictly speaking – than there was after 1945.

Many people were aware that the war had created tremendous opportunities, and that mankind had been given a challenge. They thought in broader terms. It was as if the areas of devastation had suddenly opened up immense vistas. Dark corners of life, such as the plight of the poor in large urban areas, were suddenly exposed to the light of day. Class distinction was seen as a worthless sham, and the old-style capitalist system took a severe knock. The bombs may well have destroyed the only home many people knew, but it gave the planners a chance which, in London, at any rate, they had not had since the Great Fire of 1666. How far they rose to that challenge may be judged by looking at the often sad state of our cities today.

Another cause which emerged with great vigour early in the war was that of European unity. As early as 5th October, 1939, Rose Macaulay had written in a postscript to a letter: "I am fighting for the establishment of a supreme authority in Europe whose laws and judgements shall be accepted by all European nations." This is far from complete supranational integration on the lines seen as the ultimate goal of the present Treaty of Rome, but such ideas were very latent during the early years of the war.

In an effort to hold on, it was even suggested that France and England should become one nation. The vision shimmered for a moment and then was rudely dispelled, and the French were made to look the villains of the piece. It is even more sad that Roosevelt and Churchill treated General de Gaulle so badly. The Frenchman was of course a difficult person at the best of times, but he never really forgave the Anglo-Saxons – as he liked to think of America and Britain – and, like the elephant, he never forgot. This is no attempt to exonerate the French entirely. The *Entente Cordiale* has always been a somewhat episodic affair.

Economic Peace Aims, published in London in 1941, envisaged American and European co-operation after the war, with the following aims: (1) A federal European authority controlling inter-state affairs, foreign policy, finance, commerce and industry. (2) An international commission for the procuration of work. (3) Guaranteed work and wages for all. (4) A European currency. (5) Free trade within an area which would at first consist of Europe, the British Empire and the United States. (6) Complete freedom of movement for individuals in this area. In some respects it is surprising how many of these aims were prophetic, and are on the way to being fully realized. On the other hand, some of them are as far from being realized today as they were thirty years ago. Many people imagined a united Europe after the war was over. But one must assume that in many cases it was a reflex action similar to the one which made people so friendly towards each other. Like that phenomenon, it also faded overnight.

Where did it go? It seems to have been submerged in the very real hardship of the immediate post-war years. The Festival of Britain of 1951 was a determined attempt to show that Britain was going to be the same as ever, only one assumes, better. There was no longer much thought for Europe. Britain was certainly not psychologically ready to go into Europe when Harold Macmillan was prime minister.

"When," my French friends would ask, "is England going to espouse her century?" It was a good question. In the meantime almost another ten years have been lost, and it now seems virtually too late. Returning to live in this country a few years ago, the author was shocked to find that many English people had not the faintest idea what had been taking place in Europe. They had little information at their disposal, and – worse – were unconcerned to have it. The British Press fatuously speculated as to whether Queen Elizabeth II might become Queen of Europe.

"Our main defect I take to be our leadership. No serious effort has been made to seek out able young men, and the conduct of the war is accordingly in the hands of a small bunch of elderly self-seeking men quite out of touch with modern trends . . .". This was Cecil King writing towards the end of 1940. King had tried very hard to get himself into official work – for example, at the Ministry of Information. As a professional propagandist he was dismayed that in World War Two Britain was actually behind the standard she had set herself in World War One. The leadership – or lack of it – was a fixation for him, and a regular theme in the newspapers with which he was associated. He saw no alternative to the parliamentary system, but saw a crisis of leadership. If anything, the problem is even more acute today, and a common plight of the Western world. He saw parallels between Britain and France and the Austro-Hungarian Habsburg Empire. But he commented: "I hope our fate will not be so tragic – or so ignominious." On the other hand, King analysed the Churchill phenomenon, and a month later came to this conclusion:

"I should say that politically he is a Victorian parliamentarian, and starts from the assumption that the House of Commons (and the present House of Commons at that) is the only source of political power, and that therefore anyone with any political capacity or ambition is necessarily there. Personally (or emotionally) Churchill *is* wartime England – England with all its age, its waning virility, its dogged courage, its natural assumption that instinct is more reliable than intellect. In Churchill the country feels it is personified, and for this reason there can be no question of his departure until after complete defeat. . . . His speeches are popular . . . because they are the articulate expression of what is in most Englishmen's hearts. He has no contribution to make to our future, but he personifies our present and our past."

Cecil King had many dealings with the prime minister at this time, because Churchill felt that the former's papers were being unpatriotic, and took their criticisms very hard. King went to great lengths to justify himself to Churchill, and to show that this was not so. But in saying that Churchill had no contribution to make to the nation's future, Cecil King was perfectly correct – both in relation to his war government and his post-war return to power. That administration was no more than a nostalgic afterglow in the sky after the sun had set. Constructive policies were sadly wanting.

There were, however, the children of the war – many of whom are only now beginning to find their ways into the corridors of power. The statistics tell us how healthy they were, despite the war. Interruptions in schooling had brought about a marked increase in juvenile delinquency. The number of convictions concerning young persons under seventeen in England and Wales rose by more than a third from 1939 to 1941. Malicious damage rose by seventy per cent, and petty theft by two hundred per cent. But for other young people the war had brought a great opening up of horizons. Michael Stapleton was suddenly off to Africa with the Merchant Navy. It was no joy ride. More than a quarter of the men in the Merchant Navy at the outbreak of war had either been killed or disabled by the end of it, and in 1939 pay was less than ten pounds a month – including danger money.

Did the war have any real and lasting effect on the younger generations? One would like to think that there is more universal tolerance and compassion. There has, it is true, been a resurgence of nationalism in some areas, but this is not the imperialistic nationalism of the first few decades of this century. It is universally recognized – if not always practised – that countries cannot go to war for territorial aggrandisement. Whether cold wars and nuclear arms races are to be preferred is debatable.

One thing is certain, however: war is no longer a subject for romance. It is easy to romanticize what happened between 1939 and 1945, and it is just as easy to pour scorn on the whole thing, especially in this disenchanted age. There was certainly incompetence, and the nation at large might have been spared some of the suffering and the tragedy. Worse, perhaps, those responsible calmly acknowledged the fact. Malcolm Macdonald, Minister of Health, said in the House of Commons on 9th October, 1940: "I have never denied that a great deal of the criticism [of his department's post-raid services] which was offered was entirely justified . . . I accept full responsibility for the mistakes that were made. In the first place I did leave it too much to the local authorities, and in the second place I think our circulars ... did suggest a provision which was too low in centres where, as it turned out, people had to spend considerably longer than the forty-eight hours originally anticipated."

For a very English summing up – English because of its understatement and the almost diffident quality which foreigners occasionally regard as hypocrisy – here once more is Rose Macaulay, who had been asked to broadcast to America at the beginning of January, 1941. In a few lines she seems to bring together the essential features of the war, and the Blitz in particular, for those who lived through it:

"My talk to America is about 'Consolations of the War.' I am mentioning ruin-seeing, the beauty of the black nights and the moonlit ones, the romantic scenes during raids (fire lighting the sky, *etc.*), increased companionableness, shelter life, the pleasure of waking up still alive each day. The foreigners among us, and the sympathy of the Americans. Someone just home from New York told me that Americans didn't like us to be so pompous and grand about the war, so I've tried not to be. People too often are, with all this 'Christian civilization' business and self-praise. I've tried to sound humble, and not once said 'we can take it'."

The War in Pictures

CONTENTS OF ILLUSTRATIONS

1. In Defence of the Nation

London (1) – and indeed the whole of the nation – prepared itself for the storm to come from the German forces massed on the other side of the Channel (2). The R.A.F. (3, 4 and 5) fought against tremendous odds, and played a crucial part in the early stages of the war. On the ground, Observer Corps posts (6) tracked the progress of enemy aircraft and searchlights (7) lit up the sky at night whenever there was trouble. Fire watching (8) became a familiar duty, especially in the large cities, and fire fighting, whether done professionally by the National Fire Service (9) or on a volunteer basis (10), was an almost constant activity during the Blitz.

During the air raids on London the underground railway was a favourite place of refuge for many Londoners (11), whilst the A.R.P. carried out their wide variety of duties up above them (12). Another organization of non-combattant man-power was the Home Guard (13), though how effective they would have been in the event of an invasion can never be known.

Defence meant various things to different members of the population. For some it meant covering their window panes with strips of gummed paper to reduce the danger of flying glass, and fitting blackouts (14). Gas masks were issued to everyone (15); pots and pans were turned into Spitfires (16); waste paper was salvaged (17), and car headlights were carefully masked and the vehicles themselves rendered immobile, when not in use, so as to prevent spies or airborne invaders making off with them (18).

4

5

8

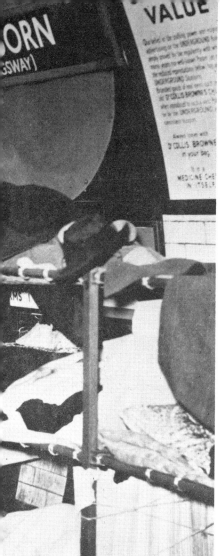

11

12

14

15

17

2. Air Raids

The development of aircraft in the inter-war period meant that in World War II the potential for terror and destruction was brought to an unprecedented level, particularly in urban areas (1). The London docks were easy and early targets for German bombers (2 and 3), and from there the raids went westwards into the City (4) and Westminster. Both St Paul's Cathedral (5) and Westminster Abbey (6) were hit, but miraculously neither was destroyed. Coventry Cathedral (7) was a direct hit, and the raid on Coventry as a whole served to emphasise how much more difficult it was for smaller cities to survive air raids than it was for such a large area as London.

Of course London had the underground (8 and 9), though it turned out to be less safe than people had imagined. Anderson shelters (10 and 11), for those who had room to erect them, were remarkably successful in saving lives, and narrow escapes became one of the talking points of the war (12 and 13). The determination to carry on as normal repeatedly burst through the devastation (14 and 15) and as long as the local pub survived (16), life was bearable for many people.

Disasters happened all the same, and no amount of bravery could bring back the dead. Amidst the ruins and the rubble, the business of clearing up the mess (17) and salvaging whatever possessions were left provided a certain amount of distraction, and a new sort of playground for the young came into being. Official artists recorded the grim scenes for posterity (18).

2

3

5

6

7

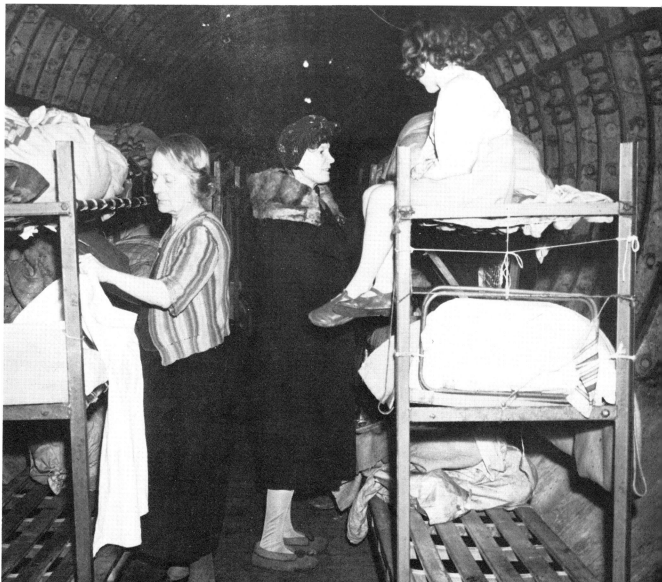

8

16

17

3. Evacuation

One of the Government's safety measures for cutting down the potential number of casualties was evacuation of as many people as possible from heavily populated areas. In practice this meant mothers and children first of all, and many of them were sent out to safer places in the country (1 and 2). In carrying out this operation during the "Phoney War", the Government acted too hastily. Moreover, the sudden confrontation between urban and rural traditions caused problems. Sometimes things went quite well (3, 4 and 5) – though this seemed to be mainly when mothers did not accompany their children. At other times evacuation did not work so well, even if the children of the same family were all able to go to the same house (6).

It was therefore almost inevitable that after the initial scare evacuees should drift back in large numbers, particularly if mothers had accompanied their children. The Government was obliged to run an advertising campaign to attempt to reverse the trend (7). In some cases the unfortunate experiences of rural families made them reluctant to take town children, especially when their standards of hygiene and general behaviour left much to be desired. Once more, the Government attempted to help by advertisements (8), though in the long run they could have requisitioned accommodation. On the other side of the coin, some evacuees still remember their host families, or the place to which they were evacuated, with great affection, and look back to that period as a happy time.

5

6

7

Thank you, Foster=Parents . . . we want more like you!

Some kindly folk have been looking after children from the cities for over six months. Extra work? Yes, they've been a handful!... but the foster-parents know they have done the right thing.

And think of all the people who have cause to be thanking the foster-parents. First, the children themselves. They're out of a danger-zone — where desperate peril may come at any minute. And they're healthier and happier. Perhaps they don't say it but they certainly mean "Thank you".

Then their parents. Think what it means to them!

The Government are grateful to all the 20,000 people in Scotland who are so greatly helping the country by looking after evacuated children. But many new volunteers are needed—to share in the present task and to be ready for any crisis that may come. Won't you be one of them? All you need do is enrol your name with the local Authority. You will be doing a real service for the nation. You may be saving a child's life.

The Secretary of State, who has been entrusted by the Government with the conduct of evacuation, asks you urgently to join the Roll of those who are willing to receive children. Please apply to your local Council.

DONT TELL
AUNTY & UNCLE

OR
COUSIN
JANE

AND
CERTAINLY
NOT——

G. LACOSTE

1

4. Propaganda and Communications

Propaganda played a major part in World War II, as indeed it had already done so in Germany during Adolf Hitler's rise to power. The humorous twist given to posters advocating control of careless talk (1, 2 and 3) and the brilliant work of such cartoonists as David Low (4) probably made more impact on the British people than the more jingoistic efforts of Government attempts at propaganda (5 and 6).

Advertising quickly managed to find a wartime theme for almost everything, including censorship (7), though newspapers exercised voluntary censorship and continued to appear (8), even when things were at their worst. Freedom of speech was never suppressed during the war. Speakers' Corner continued to flourish (9); conscientious objectors made their voices heard (10 and 11), and the fact that Hitler's attack on Russia found Britain another ally gave the Communists a ready-made platform (12).

Broadcasting became a vital weapon in this war of words. William Joyce, known as Lord Haw-Haw (13), broadcast German propaganda in English throughout the war. On several occasions he appeared to have extremely accurate sources of information, which made his broadcasts morbidly compulsive listening. Even so, the BBC established a world-wide reputation for accurate and truthful broadcasting (14). In Britain there was never anything comparable to the involvement of German youth in the war, but this row of happy British children (15) underlines the grim reality that had involved the entire nation.

A MAIDEN LOVED
AN IDLE WORD
A COMRADE LOST
AND ADOLF SERVED

2

TITTLE TATTLE LOST THE BATTLE

3

ALL BEHIND YOU, WINSTON

'LET US
GO FORWARD
TOGETHER'

BACK THEM UP!

GUINNESS IS GOOD FOR YOU

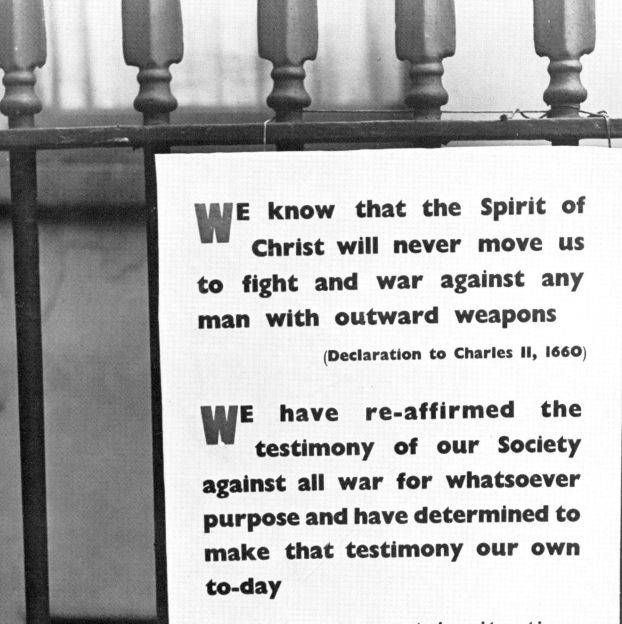

WE know that the Spirit of Christ will never move us to fight and war against any man with outward weapons

(Declaration to Charles II, 1660)

WE have re-affirmed the testimony of our Society against all war for whatsoever purpose and have determined to make that testimony our own to-day

Peace is not a certain situation, it is a condition of life, and unless Peace is rooted in God it cannot exist

(Yearly Meeting of Society of Friends, Nov. 1938)

Published by the Friends Peace Committee, Friends House, London, N.W.1; and also obtainable from the Northern Friends Peace Board, Friends Meeting House, Woodhouse Lane, Leeds, 2

12

13

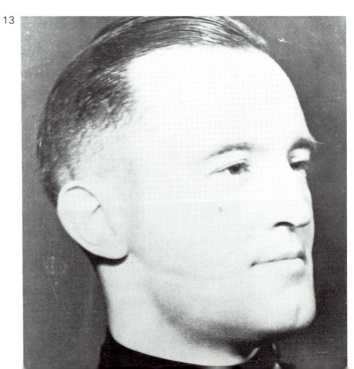

USE SPADES NOT SHIPS

GROW YOUR OWN FOOD

AND SUPPLY YOUR OWN COOKHOUSE

5. Feeding the Fighting Nation

A huge effort was made by the Government to cope with the problem of providing food for the nation. Posters emphasised how much Britain relied on imported foodstuffs (1), and therefore how necessary it was for people to grow as much as possible (2) and Dig for Victory (3). The Ministry of Food gave detailed – and often unintentionally humorous – advice to housewives on how to provide a balanced diet under wartime conditions and with rationing in force (4 and 5). Great stress was placed on the virtues of vegetables (6), and the rabbit (7), as a source of food. Officially approved ration packages were not particularly appetising (8), and it became increasingly rare to see such exotic items as bananas on open sale (9) as the war progressed.

Some families solved their problems by eating together, thus making their meagre ration go a little further (10). For poorer families, where bread was a fundamental part of the diet (11), rationing was a serious problem. Restaurants continued as best they could (12), although initially the rationing restrictions scarcely affected them, and this was the cause of some wry and even bitter comment in the Press. Firms producing food and drink managed to give their advertisements a patriotic flavour (13), though they were not always so patriotic in what they sold the public.

Feeding the forces, whether at home (14) or abroad and in prisoner-of-war camps (15), was something to which the British devoted considerable effort. Despite the loss of lives and ships, food convoys got through, and much needed supplies, such as eggs from America (16), reached this country in safety.

.. every available piece of land must be cultivated

GROW YOUR OWN FOOD
supply your own cookhouse

DIG FOR VICTORY

3

GROUP I

DY BUILDING

FOODS

These build the
body and prevent
the tissues
wearing out

Milk, Cheese, Eggs are rich
in bone-forming materials
They are particularly important
for growing children

GREEN VEGETABLES & SALADS
help you to resist infection, clear the
skin, and take the place of raw fruit.

Rabbits can be fed on

Hedgerow Weeds · **Garden Waste** · **Kitchen Scraps**

Hedge Parsley	Brussels Sprout Stems	Pot Scrapings
Plantain	Lettuce Leaves	Table Scraps
Sow Thistle	Cabbage Leaves	Root Peelings
Dandelion	Waste Potatoes	Fish Waste
Groundsel	Lawn Mowings	Pea Pods

PRINTED FOR H.M. STATIONERY OFFICE BY MULTI MACHINE PLATES LTD. LONDON E.C.4 51-2529

MACONOCHIE'S
MEAT AND VEGETABLE
RATION
with
PEAS
MACONOCHIE BROS., LTD
MACONOCHIE
LONDON, ENGLAND
PACKED 6/40

This ugly mug, yet to be made

    Commemorates the end

Of one more mug who sunk his land

    And couldn't name a friend

But meanwhile (till the mug is made)

    We'll drink in glasses clear

Our firm resolve to win the day

    In Bulmers golden cheer

Bulmer's Cider

5   2½ lbs. of apples to every flagon

H. P. BULMER & CO., LTD., HEREFORD.   103di 941x

30 DOZEN EGGS

THE CUDAHY PACKING CO.

16

1

6. Women at War

For many women the war meant the absence of the husband and father of the family – a gap which even the bravest eldest son could scarcely be expected to fill (1). As the war began to make its effect felt more keenly, people adjusted their daily life to new situations, and the determination to carry on as normal a life as possible carried many people through the worst moments of the war (2). Many women who had experienced World War I (3) were able to face the next one with a certain amount of equanimity, despite the fact that the experts forecast disaster on a huge scale.

As in World War I, women took on work that was normally done by men. They became skilled in welding (4 and 5); repairing tanks (6 and 7), and working the land (8 and 9). They joined the services and were decorated for bravery (10), and supplemented the police force (11). Society women volunteered to serve as waitresses in soldiers' canteens, as in this one in the crypt of St Martin's in the Fields in London (12). Possibly the most underestimated body of women in the whole of the war effort was the Women's Voluntary Service (13), whose omnipresence and ability to cope became legendary. In the circumstances, it seems rather hard that the responsibility for the sharp increase in venereal disease should have been blamed solely on women in the Government's poster (14). The war brought a temporary relaxation of sexual morality into almost every walk of life, and women were by no means the only ones to blame.

4

5

8

10

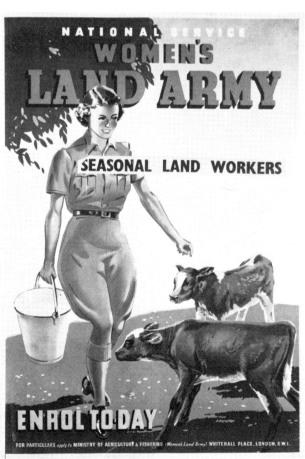

9

VD

Hello boy friend, coming MY way?

The 'easy' girl-friend spreads Syphilis and Gonorrhœa, which unless properly treated may result in blindness, insanity, paralysis, premature death

IF YOU HAVE RUN THE RISK, GET SKILLED TREATMENT AT ONCE. TREATMENT IS FREE AND CONFIDENTIAL

14

7. Entertainment in Wartime

Theatres and cinemas, along with other places of entertainment, were hit badly at the beginning of the war by the government regulations, which were based on a policy of avoiding large concentrations of people. The regulations severely restricted hours of opening and the size of gatherings. Sunday showings of films became popular, and people queued (1) to see such Hollywood favourites as Mae West (2) and British stars such as Leslie Howard (3). As officials realised how vital entertainment was for morale, theatres were allowed to re-open. In London several serious plays were put on by Alec Clunes (4) and musicals by C. B. Cochrane (5) – to name only two. The lavish and colourful musicals provided a period of relaxation and escape from the all too grim realities of war.

For those who could not get to London, favourite stars such as Leslie Henson (6) toured the country, performing in military camps and factories. Chamber music was heard where it had probably never been heard before (7), but it was probably the BBC who provided entertainment for most people. Producers such as Val Gielgud (8) directed plays, the irrepressible Tommy Handley (9) with his variety show ITMA cheered up the nation, and Vera Lynn – the forces' sweetheart – poured out scores of songs (10). Songs were also a means of raising national morale. Here "We're Gonna Hang out the Washing on the Siegfried Line" has a prominent and permanent place in a London nightclub (11).

1

3

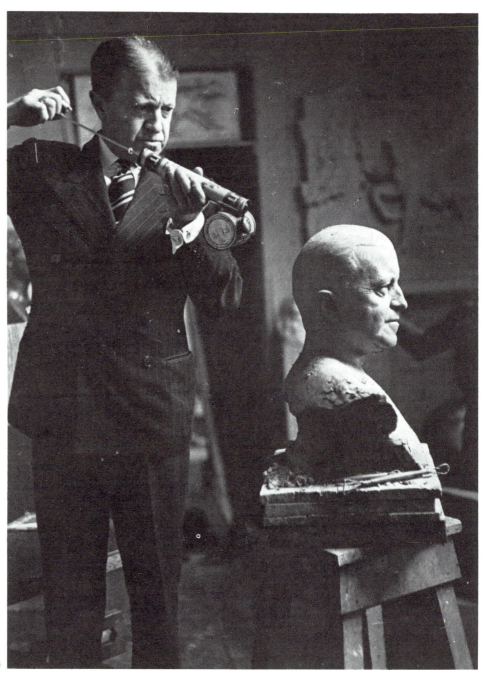

9

MARK

SHOW HER

YOUR

BLOCK BUSTER

BIBLIOGRAPHY

Baily, L.	*BBC Scrapbook*, Vol. II, 1918–39, London 1968
Bowen, E.	*The Heat of the Day*, London 1949
Briggs, A.	*A History of Broadcasting in the United Kingdom*, Vol. III, *The War of Words*, London 1970
Calder, A.	*The People's War, Britain 1939–45*, London 1969
Calder, R.	*The Lesson of London*, London 1941
Churchill, W. S.	*The Second World War*, London 1948–54
Collier, B.	*The Defence of the United Kingdom*, London 1957
Connor, W.	*The English at War*, London 1941
Cudlipp, H.	*Publish and Be Damned*, London 1953.
Firebrace, A.	*Fire Service Memories*, Melrose 1949
Fleming, P.	*Invasion 1940*, London 1957
Graves, C.	*London Transport Carried On*, London 1947
Green, H.	*Caught*, London 1947
Hancock, K., and Gowing, M.	*British War Economy*, London 1949
Harrison, T., and Madge, C. (eds)	*War Begins at Home*, London 1940
Idle, E. D.	*War over West Ham*, London 1945
Kavanagh, E.	*Tommy Handley*, London 1949
King, C.	*With Malice toward None*, London 1970
Lampe, D.	*The Last Ditch*, London 1968
Landau, R.	*The Wing*, London 1945

Macaulay, R.   *Letters to a Sister*, London 1964
Matthews, W. R.   *St Paul's Cathedral in Wartime*, London 1946

Nicolson, H.   *Diaries and Letters* Vol. I, 1930–39 and Vol. II, 1939–45, London 1966 and 1967

O'Brien, T. H.   *Civil Defence*, London 1955

Postan, M. M.   *British War Production*, London 1952

Rawnsley, C. F. and Wright, R.   *Night Fighter*, London 1968 (Paperback)

Sansom, W.   *Westminster in War*, London 1947
Strachey, J.   *Post D*, London 1941

Titmuss, R. M.   *Problems of Social Policy*, London 1950

Woon, B.   *Hell Came to London*, London 1945
Worsley, F.   *Itma*, London 1948

INDEX

ACKNOWLEDGEMENTS

The author would like to thank Michael Stapleton for his generosity in allowing him to use his wartime memoirs which form the sequel to his novel *The Threshold;* to the Rev. R. H. Hawkins, sometime Canon of Windsor, for permission to read and quote from his mother's letters, and also to the staff of the Windsor branch of the Berkshire County Library for their help and determination in tracking down books. Thanks are also due to the following author's, agents and publishers for permission to quote from their works: Messrs Jonathan Cape Ltd for Elizabeth Bowen's *The Heat of the Day* and Angus Calder's *The People's War;* Messrs Cassell & Co. Ltd for Sir Winston Churchill's *Their Finest Hour;* Messrs Collins for Harold Nicolson's *Diaries and Letters;* the Controller of Her Majesty's Stationery Office for *Report of the Chief Medical Officer of the Ministry of Health on the State of the Public Health during Six Years of War;* Messrs Faber & Faber Ltd for Rom Landau's *The Wing;* Messrs Macmillan & Co. Ltd for Edith Sitwell's *The Canticle of the Rose;* Messrs A. D. Peters & Co. for Rose Macaulay's *Letters to a Sister* (edited by Constance Babington Smith); Messrs Sidgwick & Jackson Ltd for Cecil King's *With Malice Toward None;* The Times Newspaper Limited; Messrs George Weidenfeld & Nicolson Ltd for *Chips, The Diaries of Sir Henry Channon,* edited by Robert Rhodes James.

    The author and publishers would also like to thank the following for loaning pictures used in this book: Imperial War Museum, Plates 1.1–1.6, 1.8, 1.13, 1.16, 1.17, 2.9, 2.11, 2.13, 3.7, 4.1–3, 4.12–14, 5.1–3, 5.6–7, 5.16, 6.8–10, 6.14, 7.1, 7.7; Pictorial Press Ltd, plates 1.7, 1.14, 1.18, 2.1, 2.4, 2.8, 2.10, 2.17, 3.3–5, 4.8–11, 4.15, 5.4–5, 5.8, 5.12, 5.14–15, 6.2–7, 6.11–12, 7.2, 7.4–5, 7.8, 7.10–11; Radio Times Hulton Picture Library, plates 1.9–10, 1.12, 2.2–3, 5.10–11, 6.1, 7.3, 7.6, 7.9; London Transport Executive, plate 1.11; Cartoon by David Low (plate 4.4) by arrangement with the Trustees and the London *Evening Standard;* Paul Popper Ltd, plates 2.5, 3.6; Mansell Collection, plates 2.6–7, 3.2; Central Press Agency Ltd, plates 1.15, 2.12, 2.14, 2.15 and jacket; Keystone Press Agency Ltd, plates 2.16, 2.18, 3.1, 5.9, 6.13; Stuart Durant, plates 3.8, 4.7, 5.13